Exploring
Apple Mac

Mojave Edition

Kevin Wilson

Elluminet Press

www.elluminetpress.com

Exploring Apple Mac: Mojave Edition

Publisher: Elluminet Press
Director: Kevin Wilson
Lead Editor: Steven Ashmore
Technical Reviewer: Mike Taylor, Robert Ashcroft
Copy Editors: Joanne Taylor, James Marsh
Proof Reader: Steven Ashmore
Indexer: James Marsh
Cover Designer: Kevin Wilson

eBook versions and licenses are also available for most titles. Any source code or other supplementary materials referenced by the author in this text is available to readers at

www.elluminetpress.com/resources

For detailed information about how to locate your book's resources, go to

www.elluminetpress.com/resources

Table of Contents

MacOS Mojave **12**

   What's New? 13

   Available Models 16

      Macbooks.. *16*

      iMac.. *16*

      iMac Pro *17*

      Mac Pro *17*

      Mac Mini *17*

Setting up Your Mac **18**

   Power Up 19

   Power Down 20

   Starting your Mac for the First Time 21

   Setting up Internet & WiFi 26

   Connecting Peripherals 29

   Adding Printers 31

   Apple Keys 33

      The Command Key *33*

      The Option Key *33*

      The Control Key *33*

      The Function Key *33*

   The Cloud 34

      Creating an Apple ID *34*

   Time Machine Backup 35

      Setting Up Backups *35*

      Restoring Items *39*

   System Preferences 40

   Adding Internet Accounts 42

   Additional Users 44

   Setting up Trackpads 46

Getting Around Your Mac **48**

   The Desktop 49

   Stacks 50

   The Dock 51

   Launchpad 53

   Spaces & Mission Control 54

   The Menu Bar 55

      Application Menu *55*

      Status Menu *55*

   Finder 56

      Tabs & Tags *57*

      Finder View Style *59*

Markup *61*
Smart Folders *63*
Quick Preview Files *64*
Compress Files *64*
Accessing External Drives *65*
Accessing Data CDs and DVDs *66*
Connect to a Shared Folder *67*
Sharing Files on a Network *68*
iCloud Drive 70
iCloud Drive File Sharing *73*
Managing App Windows 76
Moving a Window *76*
Resizing a Window *77*
Minimise, Maximise & Close a Window *78*
Dashboard 79
Spotlight Search... 80
Notification Centre 81
Dynamic Desktop... 85
Handoff... 86
Universal Clipboard.. 88
Instant HotSpot... 89
Using Siri 90
Apple Pay 91
Setup *91*
Using Apple Pay on your Mac................................... *94*
Auto Unlock 95
The Mac Keyboard.. 97
Useful Keyboard Shortcuts....................................... 98
MacOS Startup Keys 99
Making Gestures.. 100
One Finger Point and Tap... *100*
Two Finger Scroll.. *101*
Two Finger Rotate *101*
Two Finger Swipe *102*
Four Finger Open Launchpad................................... *102*
Magic Mouse 103
Left Click.. *103*
Right Click *103*
Scrolling... *104*
Swipe.. *104*
Find your Mouse Pointer 105
The Touch Bar 106
Touch Bar Layout *106*
Control Strip.. *107*
Application Strip *107*
Customise Touch Bar.. *109*

Dark Mode 110
Find my Mac 111
    Setup *111*
    Locating & Taking Action... *112*
Pairing Bluetooth Devices.. 113

Using Applications **114**

Launching Your Applications... 115
Killing Unresponsive Apps... 117
App Store 118
Tabbed Apps 120
Maps.. 121
    Getting Directions *121*
    Explore in 3D.. *123*
Apple Books.. 124
Notes 127
iCal Calendar.. 129
    Adding an Event... *129*
    Add an Event from Email *130*
    Subscribing to Public Calendar *131*
    Sharing Calendars & Creating Public Calendars....... *132*
Image Capture 133
Photobooth.. 134
DVDs & Blu-rays 136
Voice Memos.. 138
    Recording Memos *139*
    Renaming Memos *140*
    Trim a Memo.. *141*
News 142
Pages App 144
    Starting Pages *144*
    Formatting Text *146*
    Adding a Picture... *147*
    Instant Alpha.. *148*
    Saving... *149*
Keynote App.. 150
    Editing a Slide *151*
    Adding a New Slide... *151*
    Adding Media *152*
    Animations *153*
    Formatting Text Boxes.. *154*
    Formatting Text Inside Textboxes............................... *155*
    Adding Styles to Textboxes *156*
    Saving... *158*
Numbers App 159
    Building a Spreadsheet.. *161*
    Entering Data *161*

Changing Data Types..*162*
Adding Formulas..*162*
Adding Functions...*163*
Saving..*163*

Internet, Email & Communications................................. **164**

Using Safari to Browse the Web.............................. 165
Launching Safari...*165*
Using Safari...*166*
Bookmarking Pages..*166*
Using the Sidebar *167*
Downloads...*168*
Apple Mail.. 169
Writing an Email...*170*
Formatting your Message.......................................*170*
Add an Emoji...*171*
Add Attachment..*171*
Add Photo from Photos App *172*
Mail Drop *172*
Mail Markup *174*
Dealing with Spam & Junk Mail............................ 176
Contacts 177
Creating Groups *179*
Add Email Contact from Apple Mail *180*
Facetime 181
iMessage 184
Air Drop... 186
Mac Phone 187

Using Multimedia.. **188**

Photos App.. 189
Importing your Photos...*190*
Creating Folders and Albums...................................*192*
Adding Photos to Albums *194*
Manipulating & Enhancing Photos *195*
Adding Filters *198*
Sharing Photos *199*
Creating Photobooks...*201*
Creating Slide Shows *205*
Ordering Prints *208*
Printing Photos..*210*
Greeting Cards *212*
A Gift Calendar..*215*
Faces *217*
Places *218*
Memories *219*
Create your Own Memory..*219*

Share a Memory 222
Smart Search 223
Continuity Camera 224
iMovie 226
Importing Footage from your Camera 226
Importing Footage from your iPhone 227
Adding Clips 229
Adding Titles 230
Adding Music 231
Transitions 232
Animations 233
iTunes 234
Plugging in an iPhone or iPad 235
Add Music to iPhone or iPad 236
Burn a Playlist to a CD 237
Import from a CD 238
iTunes Store 239
Searching the Store 239
Films & TV Programmes 240
Apple Music 242
Search 244
Browse 245
Recommendations for You 246
Follow Artists 246
Creating Playlists 247
Adding Songs 247

Maintaining your Mac **248**

Firewalls 249
Gatekeeper 250
Do Apple Macs get Viruses? 251
Downloading MacOS Mojave 253
Installing MacOS Mojave 254
Create a Boot Drive 255
Booting from a USB Drive 258
Recovery Mode 262
App Updates 262
System Updates 263
SMC 264
NVRAM 265

Video Resources **266**

Index **270**

About the Author

With over 15 years' experience in the computer industry, Kevin Wilson has made a career out of technology and showing others how to use it. After earning a master's degree in computer science, software engineering, and multimedia systems, Kevin has held various positions in the IT industry including graphic & web design, building & managing corporate networks, training, and IT support.

He currently serves as Elluminet Press LTD's senior writer and director, he periodically teaches computer science at college in South Africa and serves as an IT trainer in England. His books have become a valuable resource among the students in England, South Africa and our partners in the United States.

Kevin's motto is clear: "If you can't explain something simply, then you haven't understood it well enough." To that end, he has created the Exploring Technology Series, in which he breaks down complex technological subjects into smaller, easy-to-follow steps that students and ordinary computer users can put into practice.

Acknowledgements

Thanks to all the staff at Luminescent Media & Elluminet Press for their passion, dedication and hard work in the preparation and production of this book.

To all my friends and family for their continued support and encouragement in all my writing projects.

To all my colleagues, students and testers who took the time to test procedures and offer feedback on the book

Finally thanks to you the reader for choosing this book. I hope it helps you to use your mac with greater understanding.

Have fun!

MacOS Mojave

MacOS Mojave 10.14 (pronounced "Mo-hah-vee"), is the fifteenth major release of Apple's desktop operating system for Macintosh computers.

Macs come in different shapes and sizes.

- Mac mini
- Macbook series
- iMac series
- iMac Pro series
- MacPro series

According to Apple, the following Macs will be able to support MacOS Mojave

- iMac Pro (2017 onwards)
- Mac Pro (late 2013 onwards)
- MacBook Pro (mid 2012 onwards)
- MacBook Air (mid 2012 onwards)
- MacBook (early 2015 onwards)
- iMac (late 2012 onwards)
- Mac Mini (late 2012 onwards)

Keep this in mind if you're upgrading from a previous version of MacOS.

What's New?

Mojave looks very much like its predecessors, El Capitan, Yosemite, and Sierra with a few minor interface refinements.

Mojave brings over several iOS apps such as Stocks, News and Voice Memos, as well as Emojis for email.

Apple have enhanced the 'Dark Mode' feature, making it easier on the eyes especially when using your Mac for long periods of time.

Finder has a new gallery view, and Quickview has a few more features such as markup

Chapter 1: MacOS Mojave

Users can organise cluttered icons by automatically stacking files into groups based on file attribute. Just click on a stack to view the files.

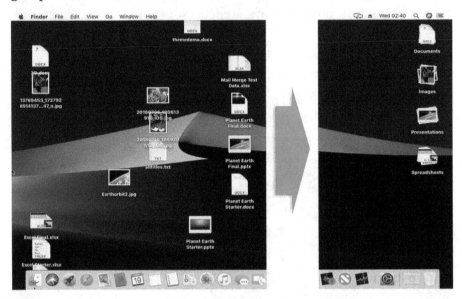

A new feature called Dynamic Desktop adjusts the desktop wallpaper according to the time of the day...

The dock also now has a 'recent apps' section on the right hand side.

Mac App Store has been rewritten from the ground-up and now features a new interface similar to the App Store on iPhone/iPad. A new 'Discover' tab highlights new and updated apps.

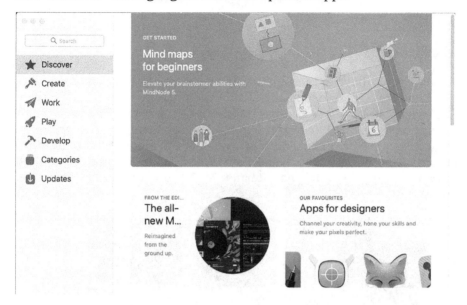

Now you can use your iPhone or iPad to take a picture or scan a document, and have it automatically appear on your mac with a new feature called continuity camera.

Available Models

Lets take a closer look at the different Macs available from the Apple Store.

Macbooks

Currently you have a choice between the Macbook, Macbook Pro, and MacBook Air. The Macbook is a smaller machine with a 12" screen. The Macbook Air offers two models, both 13" screens. The only major difference is, the higher model offers a slightly faster processor, touch ID and larger hard disk. The Macbook and Macbook Air are great for an on-the-go lifestyle as they are small and light, but are only suited to basic computing such as internet, email, photos, music, facetime, and so on.

The Macbook Pro offers more processing power and is aimed at creative types and those who use more power hungry apps such as games, video editing, music production, graphic design, and so on. The Macbook Pro offers two models: one with 13" screen and one with a 15". The higher models have the touch bar, touch ID, faster processor, and a larger hard disk.

iMac

The iMac is Apple's 'all in one' desktop computer and comes in two different models. There is one with a 21.5" inch screen and one with a 27" screen. The higher models come with a 4K or 5K retina display. All iMacs come with keyboard and mouse.

These are great for the average user and can run a variety of power hungry apps as well as internet, email, facetime, etc.

iMac Pro

The iMac Pro is similar to the iMac, except the iMac Pro is only available in a 27" 5K screen, has much faster processor and comes with an SSD drive. The iMac Pro is a dark grey colour instead of the silver on the iMac.

These machines are aimed at creative types and power users and are very fast. They are well suited to video editing, graphic design, and music production.

Mac Pro

The Mac Pro is a rather unique looking machine and is the most powerful of the Mac computers. This machine does not come with a screen, nor a keyboard and mouse - so you'll need to buy these separately.

These machines are aimed at creative types and power users and are very fast. They are well suited to video editing, graphic design, and music production.

Mac Mini

The idea behind the Mac Mini was to allow users to use their existing screen, keyboard, and mouse. It's worth noting that you will need a screen that connects to the computer using an HDMI cable.

If your screen uses VGA or DVI, you'll need an adapter to convert to HDMI.

The Mac Mini currently has two options which are identical except the higher model has a faster processor and larger hard disk.

Mac Minis are great entry level desktop machines and run as well as an iMac.

Setting up Your Mac

Setting up Mojave is pretty straight forward. If you haven't already got it installed, you can find a tutorial on page 253.

Once it is installed and ready to go, you will need to connect your WiFi or internet connection.

Create an Apple ID if you haven't already got one. If you do but didn't enter it during installation, you can sign in with your Apple ID in system preferences under iCloud.

Also it's a good idea to set up Time Machine using an external hard drive to do periodic automatic backups of your data.

To help you better understand this section, take a look at the video resources. Open your web browser and navigate to the following site:

www.elluminetpress.com/using-macos/

Power Up

The power button on the mac is on the top right of the keyboard on a MacBook laptop.

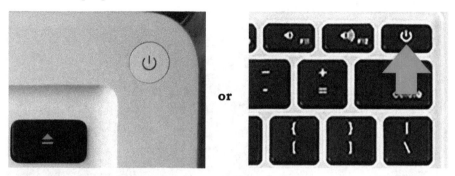

On the Macbooks with the touch bar, you can unlock and power up your Mac using the touch sensor on the top right of the keyboard.

On the iMac and Mac Mini, the power button is situated on the back panel.

Press the button once to start up your mac.

You can also use the power button to force your mac to shutdown in the event of a crash or lock up. Hold the button until the screen goes blank. Only use this option if you're having problems.

Power Down

To power down your mac or send it into sleep/standby mode, go to the apple menu on the top left of the screen...'

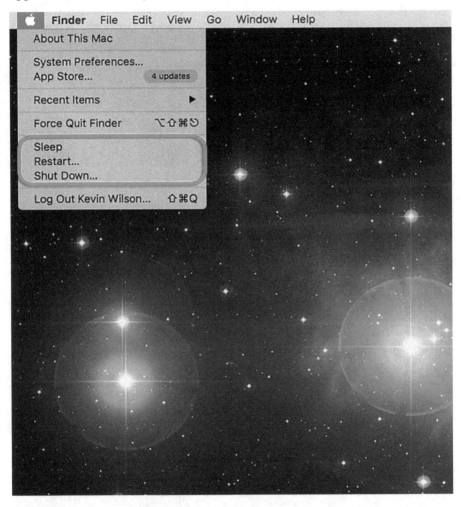

Click 'shut down' to shut down and power off your mac.

Click 'restart' to reboot your mac.

You can also click 'sleep', this will put your mac into standby mode and is convenient if you use your mac on the go a lot and don't have time to wait for your machine to start up.

If you are using a macbook laptop, you can just close the lid and your macbook will go into sleep mode.

Starting your Mac for the First Time

When you turn on a new mac for the first time, you'll need to go through some initial steps to set up wifi, select language, regional preferences and sign in with your Apple ID.

On the first screen, select your language. Click, the 'next' arrow.

Select your country of residence. Click 'continue'.

Select your keyboard layout: US for the United States, UK for United Kingdom, and so on. If you don't see yours click 'show all'. Click 'continue' when you're done.

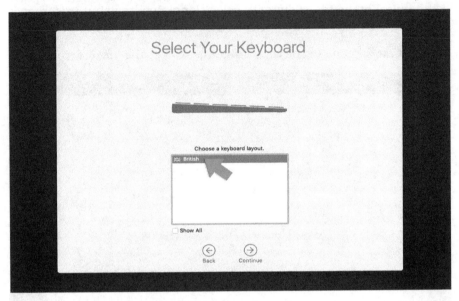

Select your WiFi network. Enter your WiFi password in the box that appears underneath. You'll find your WiFi network name and password printed on the back of your router - if not contact your internet service provider and ask them for your WiFi details.

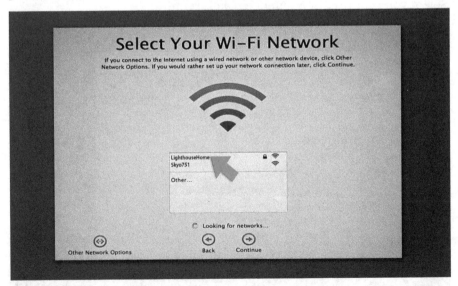

Click 'continue'.

In the next window, click 'not now' if you are setting up a clean mac. Click 'continue'.

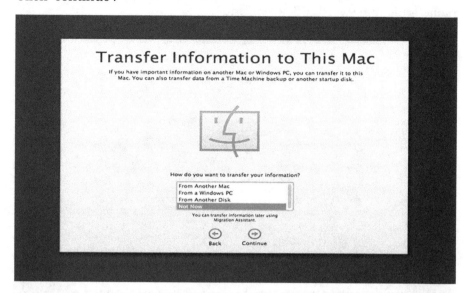

Log in with your Apple ID. This allows you to make use of apple email, iCloud, buy music, films and TV programmes, as well as Apps from the App Store.

If you don't have one click 'create a free Apple ID' and follow the instructions to enter your details. Otherwise enter your Apple ID email address and password then click continue.

Agree to the terms and conditions. Click 'use my iCloud account to log in'. This will log you into your Mac with your Apple ID. Enter your name and a password. Click 'continue'.

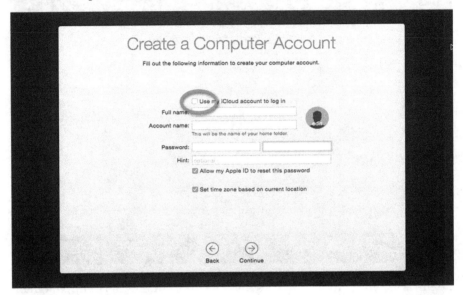

Express setup configures your mac using the most common default settings.

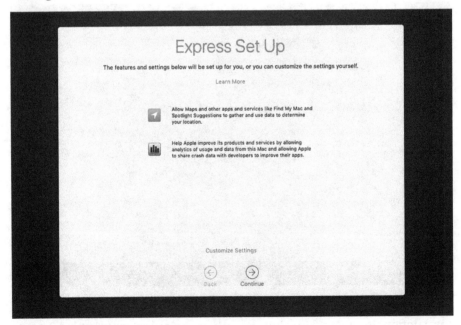

You can change these settings later on, click 'continue' for now.

Choose the 'look' you want. You can either use the light theme or the dark theme. With the light theme, backgrounds are white, toolbars are grey and the screen is a lot brighter. The dark theme uses darker colours, so the backgrounds are a dark black colour with slightly lighter toolbars and the screen is a lot easier on the eyes, especially if you use your Mac for long periods of time.

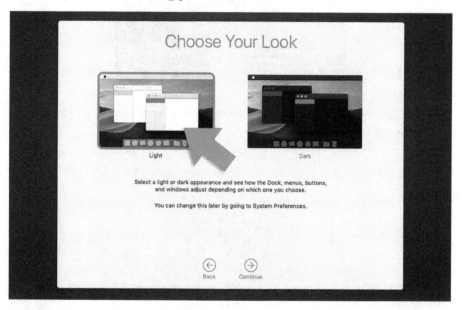

Click 'continue' and allow your Mac to set itself up.

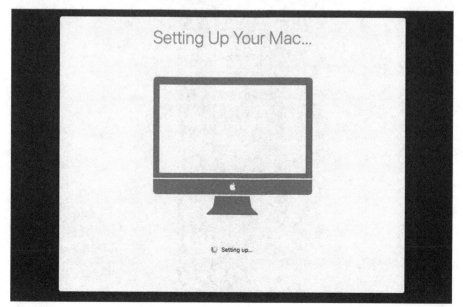

Setting up Internet & WiFi

To set up your WiFi, select the WiFi symbol on the status menu on the right hand side of the screen. From the dropdown, select your WiFi network.

In the dialog box that appears on your screen, enter the WiFi password. This is usually the network key.

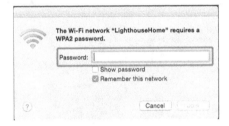

This is usually printed on the back of your modem, access point, or router and is sometimes called SSID.

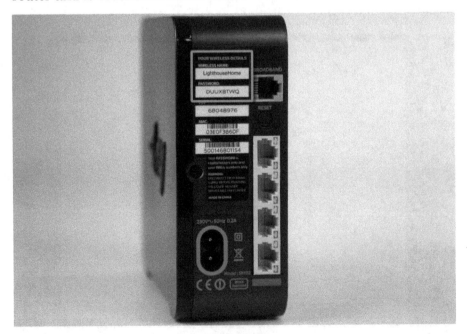

You can use the same procedure, if you are in a public hotspot eg library, coffee shop, airport and so on

If WiFi isn't available, and you use a cable modem to get online in your home, you can use a cable.

Here is a typical setup.

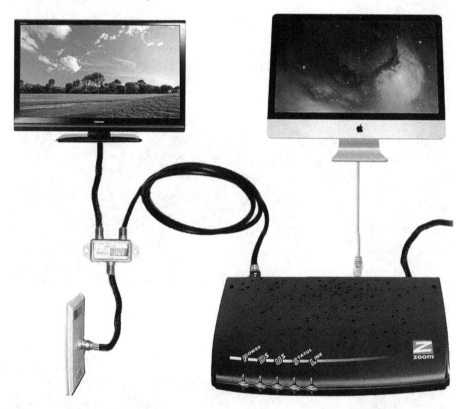

Your coax cable coming into your home is usually split using a splitter. One cable will go to your TV and the other will go to your modem.

Your computer will connect to your modem using an Ethernet cable.

Chapter 2: Setting up Your Mac

Plug one end of the Ethernet cable into your modem, then power up your modem and allow it to connect to your ISP.

Plug the other end into the Ethernet port on your computer, as shown below.

Your mac should connect automatically. To check, go to system preferences and select network.

Click on Ethernet on the left hand side, and make sure IPv4 is set to DHCP and your computer has picked up an IP address.

Connecting Peripherals

You can connect peripherals such as external drives, scanners, and printers. You connect peripherals using a USB cable. On the side panel of the MacBook, you'll find your USB ports. These will be USB-C ports, also known as thunderbolt 3. On the side panel of your macbook, you'll see these ports.

If you need standard USB ports, or HDMI, then you can get a hub that plugs into the side of your macbook.

These USB-C hubs are available at most computer stores and online.

The USB-C hub will allow you to use the USB-A type used on the most common peripherals.

On the back panel of the iMac. Here you'll see your USB ports, ethernet, headphones, and an SD card reader so you can read memory cards from digital cameras.

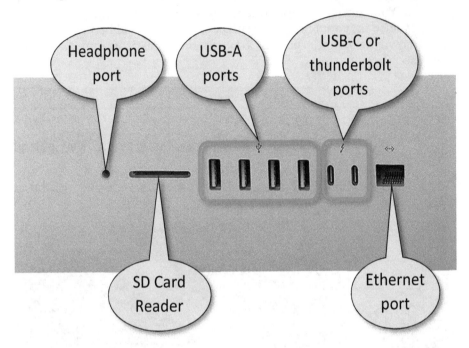

The back panel of your mac mini 2018. Here you'll find your USB ports, and HDMI port for plugging in a monitor, ethernet, and a headphone jack.

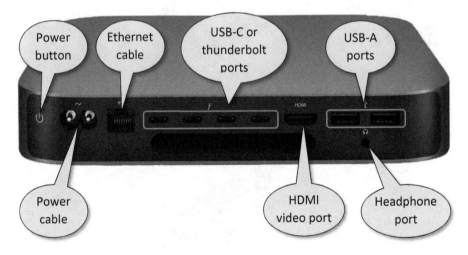

You'll also find the power buttons and power cable ports.

Adding Printers

Click on the Apple menu on the top left of your screen. From this menu, select 'System Preferences'.

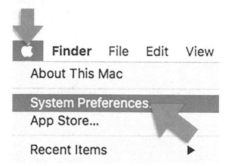

From the system preferences window, double click 'Printers & Scanners'.

Click the lock on the bottom left of the window, then enter your username and password. This is to unlock the settings.

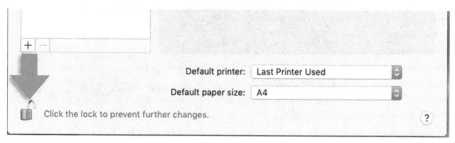

Chapter 2: Setting up Your Mac

Click on the plus sign shown above to add a printer.

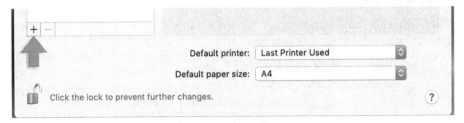

In the box that appears, MacOS will scan for connected printers; whether they are connected via USB or WiFi.

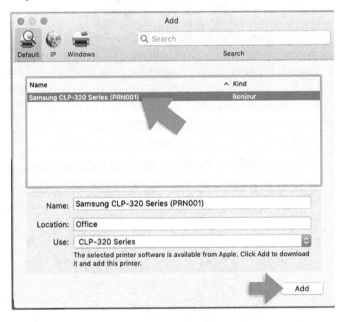

Select your printer from the list and click 'add'. Your mac will download the driver from its own driver library.

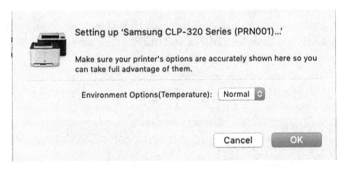

Click ok.

Apple Keys

Macs have a few special keys that allow you to carry out certain operations on your mac.

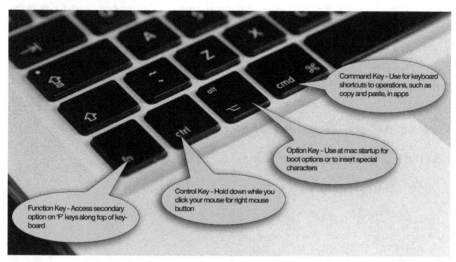

The Command Key

This is equivalent to the control key on a PC, and allows you to use keyboard shortcuts for various commands available on the menu in different applications. For example, to undo something press Command-Z, to save press Command-S to print press Command-P and so on.

The Option Key

Also known as the Alt Key, allows you to select which drive to boot from when your Mac starts. Useful if you need to boot your mac from a start-up disk.

The Control Key

This key allows you to use the right click option on your mouse.

The Function Key

This key is used to perform special functions with the 'F' keys along the top on a MacBook keyboard.

The Cloud

iCloud is an online data storage service developed by Apple. The service allows you to store data such as documents, photos, music and iOS applications on remote servers so you can access your data on your iPad, iPhone, or Mac from anywhere with an internet connection.

iCloud synchronises email, contacts, calendars, bookmarks, notes, reminders (to-do lists), iWork documents, photos and other data so you can access them from anywhere.

Creating an Apple ID

To create an Apple ID open safari and go to the website:

`appleid.apple.com`

From the website click 'Create your Apple ID' on the top right.

Fill in the form with your details, scroll down to the bottom and click 'continue'.

You will need this Apple ID if you want to purchase Apps from the App Store, use iCloud, Apple Email, or purchase songs from iTunes Store.

Time Machine Backup

The Time Machine allows you to create backups of your files to an external hard drive.

Setting Up Backups

To use Time Machine, get yourself an external hard drive. You'll need at least 500GB - 1TB in size. Connect your external hard drive to a USB port as shown below.

Go to your finder and select 'applications'. Double click on 'time machine'.

Click 'set up time machine'.

Make sure you select 'show time machine in menu bar'. From the time machine window, select 'backup automatically'.

Select your external drive. My drive is called 'datafour', so I'll select that one. The drive is usually labelled with the manufacturer's name or model. Select 'use disk'.

Make sure you use a blank external hard drive and not one that contains any important files. Time Machine will ask you if you want to erase the disk, click 'erase'.

Time Machine will now prepare your external drive for backups and backup your files. This will take a while.

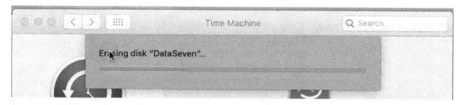

Select 'show time machine in menu bar' to allow you quick access to your backup.

Whenever you want to back up, just connect your external hard drive and the backup will start automatically. If not, click the Time Machine icon on the menu bar on the top right and select 'backup now'.

Make sure you connect your hard drive at least weekly, or daily depending on how much work you do.

When you reconnect your hard drive, click on the Time Machine icon on the menu bar at the top of the screen. Usually the backup starts automatically.

If the backup has started you'll see the progress of the backup at the top of the drop down menu.

If it hasn't started, select 'backup now' from the drop down menu.

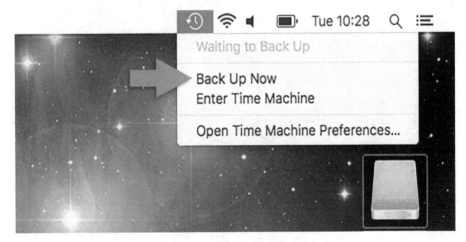

Restoring Items

To restore something click the icon on your menu bar as shown below.

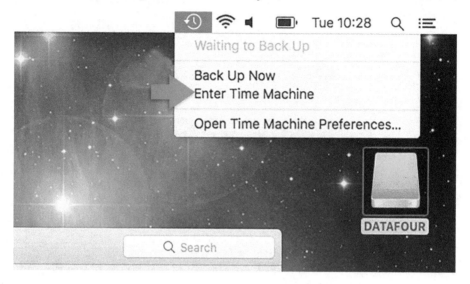

Plug in your external hard drive you used to back up.

Look for the file in the finder window shown; select what date to go back to on the left hand side using the back/forward arrows.

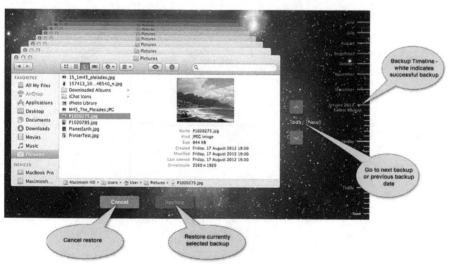

When you have found the file, click restore on the bottom right of the screen.

The file will be restored to its original location.

System Preferences

System preferences is the control panel for your mac. Here you can personalise your system and change settings.

To open your system preferences, click the Apple menu on the top left hand side of your screen, and select 'system preferences'.

Here is a brief explanation of what each of the sections in the system preferences panel does and where to go when you are looking for a setting.

Option	Description
General	Changes to the general colour scheme, light/dark mode, scroll bars, default browser.
Desktop & Screen Saver	Change desktop pictures as well as screen saver settings
Dock	Dock size, location, and effects
Mission Control	Dashboard as space or overlay, hot corners, mission control keyboard and mouse shortcuts, as well as launch pad
Language & Region	Set language, regional settings for on screen text, calendar, time formats, as well as keyboard layout preferences
Security & Preferences	File vault, gatekeeper, firewall and privacy settings. Password change for current user
Spotlight	Preferences for system wide search settings
Notifications	Notification center settings, alerts, banners and which apps are allowed send notifications.
Displays	Set display resolution, colour calibration, and multiple screen settings
Energy Saver	Set sleep times for screen, system and disk drives
Keyboard	Set keyboard shortcuts, and layout settings
Mouse	Set pointer track speed, scroll speed and double click speed
Trackpad	Set pointer track speed and sensitivity, as well as multi touch gestures
Printers & Scanners	Add printers or scanner devices, as well as device settings
Sound	Set system sound effects, microphone or speaker settings
Startup Disk	Select disk macos uses to boot
iCloud	Configure iCloud settings, account details, manage iCloud storage, and family settings
Internet Accounts	Add email accounts
Software Update	MacOS system updates
Network	Network settings for WiFi, ethernet. Adjust IP addresses, DNS and so on
Bluetooth	Pair bluetooth devices. Turn on/off bluetooth.
Extensions	Add third party extensions to photos, actions, finder, share menu etc
Sharing	Share files or a printer attached to your mac. Remote login, screen sharing and internet sharing settings.
Users & Groups	Add and delete user accounts, change passwords, auto login or user switching
Parental Controls	Manager a child's activity when using your mac
Siri	Enable/disable Siri
Date & Time	Set date and time format for different locations, time zones, etc
Time Machine	Time machine settings to back up files to an external hard disk
Accessibility	Manage screen readability, voice over, speech, etc

Whenever you need to change a setting or a preference you should come to the system preferences panel.

Adding Internet Accounts

You can add all your internet accounts such as Facebook, Twitter, iCloud and any email accounts you may have.

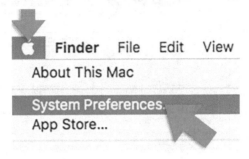

You can do this by tapping on 'Internet Accounts' in the system preferences app.

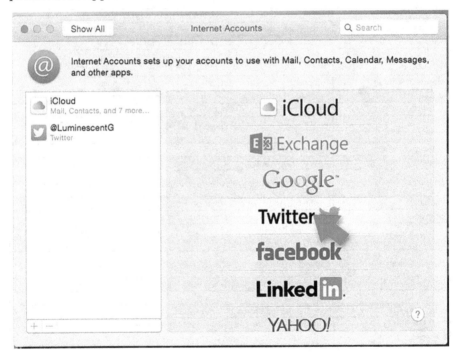

To add an account, tap the icon on the right had side. In my example, I am adding a twitter account, so tap twitter and enter login user-name and password.

When you add Facebook and Twitter accounts, each person's social media handle is added to a contact card in your address book.

Add your other email accounts too. If you have a gmail, microsoft or yahoo account, you can add them here.

In this example, I'm adding my gmail account. So click on 'google'.

Sign in with your gmail email address and password. Click 'next'.

Click the tick boxes to select what you want to sync between your mac and your gmail account. You can bring over your email, contacts, calendars and notes. All these will be added to your mail, contacts, calendar and notes apps on your mac. Click 'done' when you're finished.

Additional Users

You can create multiple user accounts for all those who use your Mac. So you could create one for each family member.

To do this, open the system preferences. Click the Apple menu on the top left, then select 'system preferences'

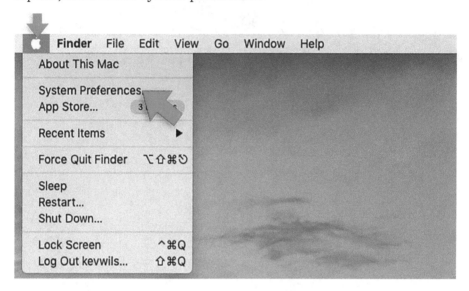

Click 'users & groups' from the 'system preferences' window.

Click the small padlock on the bottom left of the window to unlock the settings. Enter your mac username and password - the one you used to sign into your mac.

To add a new user, click the '+' sign on the bottom left.

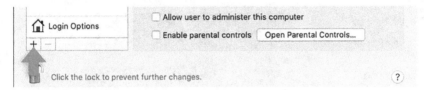

Fill in the details in the 'new user' form.

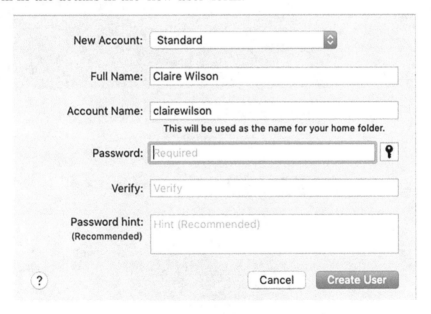

For 'new account', set it to 'standard'. Only use 'administrator' if you want to allow this user to change system settings or install apps.

Enter the user's first and second names into the 'full name' field. Your mac will automatically create an account name.

Enter a password for this account in the 'password' and then again in the 'verify' fields.

Click 'create user' when you're done.

Setting up Trackpads

Personally I find the default settings on the trackpad to be very unresponsive and hard to use. So I tweak the settings in the system preferences.

Open your system preferences. Click the Apple menu on the top left, then select 'system preferences' from the menu.

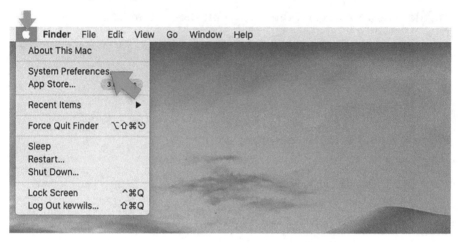

Select 'trackpad' from the system preferences window.

On the point and click tab, enable 'tap to click'. This allows you to use the tap feature to select something, rather than trying to click the left button on the trackpad.

Also turn up the tracking speed if you find the mouse pointer really slow.

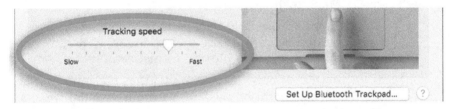

On the 'scroll & zoom' tab, un-check 'scroll direction: natural'. So when you run your fingers down the trackpad your page scrolls down with you instead of up.

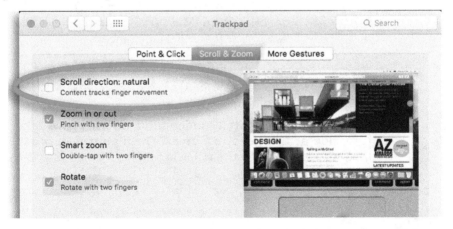

This makes it a lot easier to navigate through pages on websites and other applications.

Getting Around Your Mac

MacOS Mojave is version 10.14 and the fourteenth major release of the MacOS operating system for Macintosh computers.

Mojave's user interface isn't much different from its predecessor and still incorporates a flatter visual appearance with blurred translucent effects.

In this version, there are under the hood improvements to the Operating System, with a few visual tweaks to the interface

Mojave will run on the following systems:

- MacBook (Early 2015 or newer)
- MacBook Air (Mid 2012 or newer)
- MacBook Pro (Mid 2012 or newer)
- Mac mini (Late 2012 or newer)
- iMac (Late 2012 or newer)
- iMac Pro (2017)
- Mac Pro (Late 2013, Mid 2010 and Mid 2012 models)

To help you better understand this section, take a look at the video resources. Open your web browser and navigate to the following site:

www.elluminetpress.com/using-macos/

and

www.elluminetpress.com/mac-nav

The Desktop

The desktop is the basic working area on your mac. It's the equivalent of your workbench or office desk; hence why it is called a desktop.

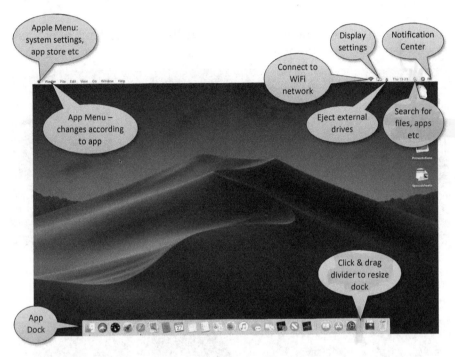

On the desktop you will find the dock along the bottom of the screen, here you can find apps to launch.

At the top of the screen you'll find your menu bar. This changes according to which app you're currently using - this is called the application menu.

On the far left hand side you'll find the apple menu, where you can access preferences, app store, log out, shut down and so on.

On the right hand side of the menu bar, you'll find status icons for your wifi, battery, display, clock, spotlight search, siri, and your notification centre. This is known as the status menu.

Stacks

Users can organise cluttered icons by automatically stacking files into groups based on file attribute - so images are stacked in one pile, documents in another, and so on.

To activate desktop stacks, right click on the desktop and select 'use stacks' from the popup menu.

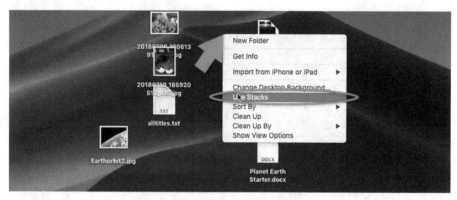

The documents will be stacked neatly on the right hand side of the screen. To open any of the stacks, just click on the icon.

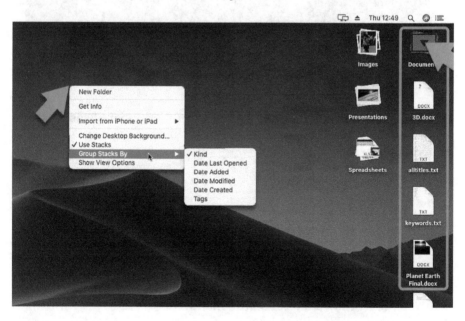

You can also group your stacks by file type (kind), date, or tags. To do this, right click on the desktop and go to 'group stacks by'. From the slide out menu, select an option and see what happens

The Dock

The dock has short cuts to applications, such as iTunes or iPhoto. If the app you are looking for isn't here, it will be in the applications folder in finder or on Launchpad.

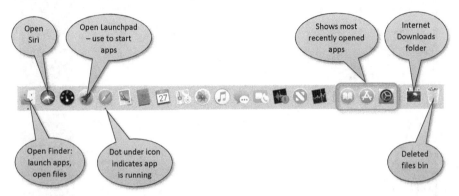

The apps along the left hand side of the dock represent apps installed on your system. You'll see the finder, siri, and Launchpad, along with a few others. Along the right hand side you'll see a divider and three apps - these are your most recently used apps and change according to the apps you use on your Mac.

The next icon on the right is your downloads stack - this is where you'll find the files you've downloaded off the internet.

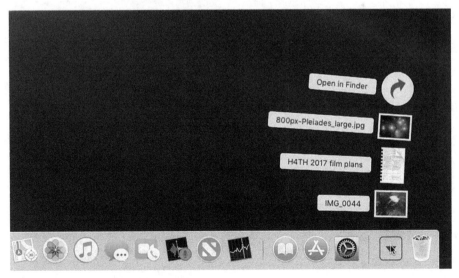

This folder is called a stack as it opens out as shown above, allowing you to see the names of the files without opening the folder.,

You can also add other folders as stacks to the right hand side of the dock. I'm going to drag my 'documents' folder from the finder window, and drop it next to the 'downloads' icon on the far right of the dock. This creates a stack.

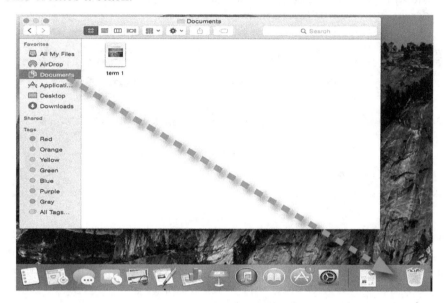

You can also add a program you use a lot to the dock. A common example is dashboard. You can drag the icon from the apps folder in finder.

I'm going to place it in between my Launchpad icon and my safari web browser icon. Just drag it to the dock.

Launchpad

Launchpad lets you see, organize, and easily open apps installed on your machine. The icons are organized into pages. To access Launchpad, click the icon on your dock, shown below. You can also press F4.

To launch any application, just click on the corresponding icon.

You can organize your applications into folders in Launchpad. Just drag and drop one icon on top of another. For example, you can drag all your reference apps together such as dictionary and calculator into a folder. When you need to find them you just click on the folder when you open launchpad.

You can also search for apps using the search field at the top of the screen.

To remove icons, click and hold your mouse button on an icon until you see a small cross appear on the top left. Click to delete app.

If you have a lot of apps installed, you will have multiple pages of apps, click the page indicators at the bottom of the screen to move between pages. You can also swipe two fingers across your macbook trackpad.

Spaces & Mission Control

If you use a lot of apps at the same time, your desktop can get a little cluttered. Mac OS has a feature called spaces, that allows you to organize apps onto different virtual desktops called a space. It's like having more than one desk in your office - different projects will be laid out on different desks. You can have a desktop that has your email and web browser open, another desktop you could be working on a keynote presentation and an accompanying report in pages, another space could have photos open and so on.

To open mission control, press F3 on your keyboard. To create new virtual desktops, click the '+' icon on the top right of the screen.

Open the apps you are going to work on. Eg safari web browsing and email.

Press F3 again. Click the '+' sign at the top right of the mission control screen to create another virtual desktop. On this desktop I'm going to work on my 'international modern architecture' project. For this project, I need pages and keynote. So I'd open these apps.

To shift between spaces swipe using 3 fingers on the trackpad on your MacBook. Or press F3 on your keyboard and click the desktop icon at the top of the screen to switch to it.

The Menu Bar

You'll find the menu bar along the top of your screen, and will look something like this:

One thing to notice about the menu bar is it changes according to which application you have showing on your screen. For example, the finder app will have its own menu, iMovie will have a different menu. Keep your eye on the top left hand side of the menu bar as it will have the name of the application currently running in bold type.

Application Menu

The left hand side of the menu bar contains the menu for the app you're currently using.

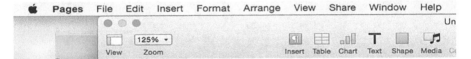

The name of the app appears in bold next to the Apple menu. There are several other app menus, often with standard names such as File, Edit, Format, Window, and Help.

Many of the commands in these menus are standard in all apps. For example, the Open command is usually in the File menu and the Copy command is usually in the Edit menu.

Status Menu

The right hand side of the menu bar contains the status menu.

This menu gives feedback on the status of your computer or give you quick access to certain features - for example; you can quickly turn on Wi-Fi, do a spotlight search, change your Mac's volume, see date & time, and check messages in notification centre.

If your menu bar is starting to get a bit crowded, you can remove items by holding down the Command key and dragging items out of the menu.

Finder

This is where all your documents, letters, photographs and favourite music are stored. The finder is like your filing cabinet.

You'll find the finder icon on the far left hand side of your dock.

Lets take a closer look at the different parts of the finder window.

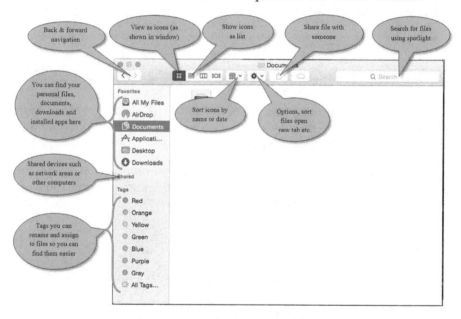

The finder window is divided into three main parts:

- The toolbar across the top of the window where you can customise the way files are displayed.

- The sidebar which you can use to choose locations and devices on your computer.

- The main contents, the large pane where all the files and folders are displayed for you to click.

Tabs & Tags

Tags allow you to place markers onto your documents to allow you to find them easier.

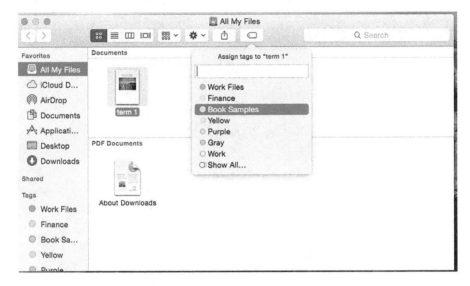

Click the document you want to tag then select the tags icon. From the list, select the tag that describes the category of your document, eg book samples, work, holiday etc.

To rename the tags to something more useful, in the Finder, click on the Finder menu, then select 'preferences'

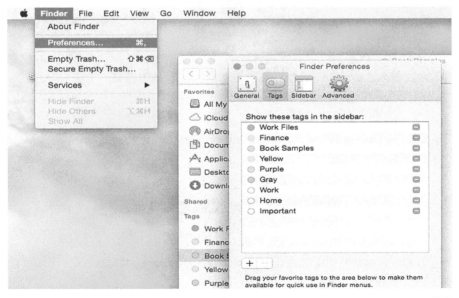

Click on the 'tags' tab at the top of the preferences window.

You will see a list of the colour tags, and a few more at the bottom such as, 'Work', 'Home', and 'Important'.

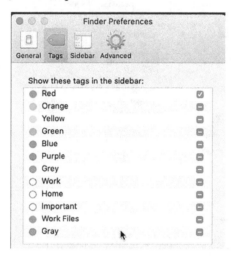

To change the colour of a tag, click on the little bubble and choose a colour.

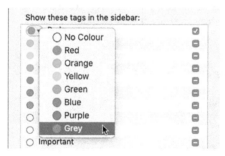

To change the name of the tag, click on the tag title, and type your new tag name.

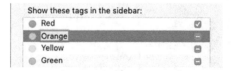

Highlight a tag in the sidebar and you will see all the folders that fall under that tag.

Finder View Style

The four icons at the top of the finder window allow you to display your file icons in different formats. You can display them as a grid of icons, or a list of icons with file details.

Icon View. This view is useful for scanning through photographs or videos. The slider on the status bar will resize the icons and previews.

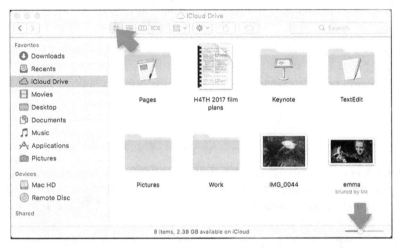

List View. This is useful for looking through documents and file names. You can sort the list according to name, size or type - just click on the column headers.

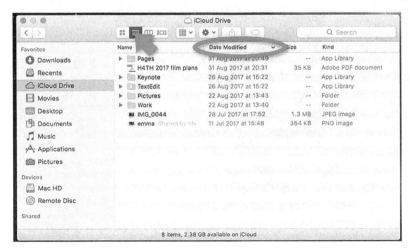

Column View. This is useful if you are looking through files that are stored in lots of folders, as you can open up the folders in each column and view the contents side by side.

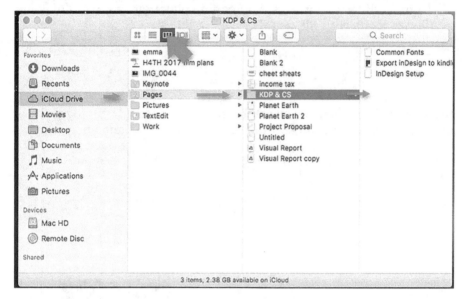

Gallery View. This is useful for scanning through photographs, videos, documents, or music. Thumbnail previews of the files appear in the bottom third of the window with a larger preview of the selected file in the top half of the window.

On the right hand side you'll see some details about the file.

Markup

Markup allows you to annotate documents and photographs just by opening up a preview, rather than opening the file in an app. You can do this from gallery view in finder. Select a document from the gallery view.

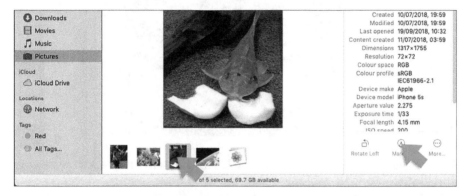

Once the markup screen appears, you can add text, shapes and colour.

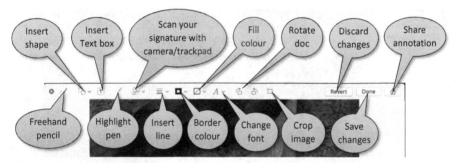

I'm going to add a shape. Click the small down arrow next to the shape icon and select a shape.

Draw the shape on the image, and double click inside it to add some text.

To change the size, colour and font, click the small down arrow next to the font icon on the toolbar. From the drop down menu, you can select a font, change the colour and size, change the typeface to bold italic or underlined, and also change the text alignment.

Click 'done' on the top right of the toolbar when you're finished. Click 'revert' to discard the annotations. Click the 'share' icon to send your file with the annotations to someone else.

Smart Folders

Smart folders can be quite useful for keeping track of files. Smart folders allow you to create search parameters and save the search as a folder; so for example, the folder displays the files you worked on in the last 30 days, or it displays all your photos and so on.

To create a smart folder, open your finder window and click the 'file' menu. From the menu select 'new smart folder'.

Now along the top of the window, you can select where you want the smart folder to search. Select 'this mac' to search your whole mac.

Now select the search criteria. This is where you tell the smart folder what you want to display in your folder.

Click in the left most drop down box where it says 'kind' and select a criteria. In the example, I want to create a folder that displays the latest files I have worked on. So select 'last opened date'.

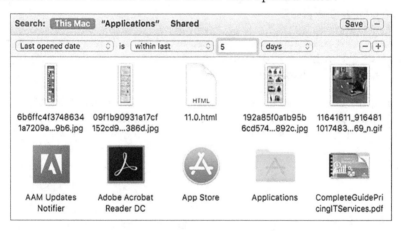

Go to the next drop down box along 'within last' and make sure its set to 'within last'.

In the text field next to it, enter the number of days. I want to show the last 5 days, so I will enter 5.

You can also set 'days' to 'weeks' or 'months' depending on what you're trying to show.

Try some of the other criteria in the first drop down box on the left.

Quick Preview Files

When browsing through your files in finder you can take a quick preview of the file. This works well with photos, documents and videos.

To preview a file, click the file to select it, then press the space bar on your keyboard. A window will popup displaying a preview version of the file.

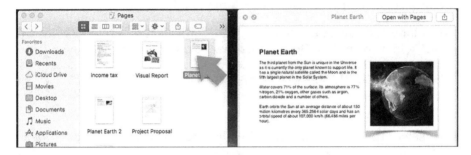

On the toolbar along the top, you can open the file in the appropriate app to edit it, or you can share the file via email or social media.

Compress Files

You can compress files into zip archives right within finder. These can be useful if you intend to send a lot of files over email, messaging or if you're making multiple files available for download.

To compress files, select them in finder - hold down the CMD key to select multiple files. Then right click on the selection, from the popup menu select 'compress items'.

You'll see a new file appear called **archive.zip**. This is the file that will contain all the files you selected. You can rename and send this file.

Accessing External Drives

When you plug in a USB flash drive or an external hard drive like the one below, an icon will appear on your desktop.

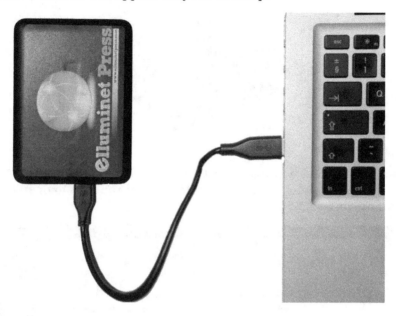

Double click this icon to open the drive in finder.

Note before unplugging the drive, it is good practice to eject the drive by clicking on the eject icon next to the drive name in finder.

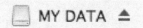

Accessing Data CDs and DVDs

Most of the new Macs no longer include DVD or CD drives. If this is the case on your Mac, you'll need to buy an external USB DVD drive.

Plug the DVD drive into a spare USB port and insert your disc. An icon will appear on your desktop. Double click on the icon to open the disc contents in finder.

Notice the DVD/CD drive is selected under 'devices' on the left hand panel of the finder window.

In the main finder window, you'll see all the files and folders contained on the disc. Double click on any of these to open them up.

To eject your disc. Click the eject icon next to the DVD/CD drive on the left hand panel in finder.

Connect to a Shared Folder

You can also connect to shared resources on a network or the internet. You can connect to a file server running both Windows Server, Linux or MacOS Server. To do this, open finder from the dock and click the 'go' menu at the top of the screen, select 'connect to server'.

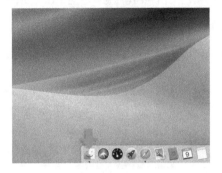

To connect to a shared folder located on a Windows server or computer, you'll need to use the smb protocol.

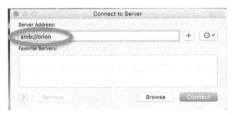

For example...

```
smb://orion/public
```

Where 'orion' is the server or computer name and 'public' is the shared folder on that server or computer. Click the plus sign on the right hand side to add the server address you just entered to the 'favorite server' list. Click 'connect' to connect to your server. You may be prompted for a username and password - this will be the username that you use to log into the server or computer you're trying to connect to, and will probably be different from the username and password you used to log onto your mac.

You can also connect to FTP servers using the same method, except use ftp:// instead followed by your FTP username, then server name.

```
ftp://kevwils@ftp.myftpserver.com
```

You'll be prompted for your username and password for that server. You can usually obtain this from your internet service provider.

Sharing Files on a Network

You can share files across your home network. This is useful if you are sharing resources such as documents with other people who are connected to your network and is ideal for transferring larger files.

To set up file sharing, open your system preferences and double click 'sharing'.

Click the padlock on the bottom left of the screen, then enter your username and password. On the left hand side turn on file sharing.

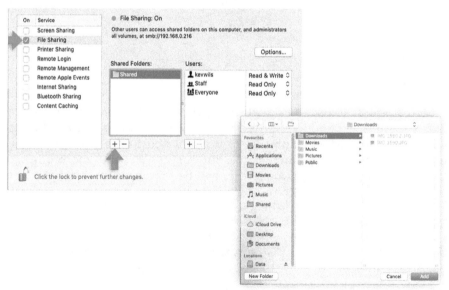

Under 'shared folders', click the plus sign and select a folder on your mac you want to share. Click 'add'.

Now select the folder you just shared under the 'shared folders' section.

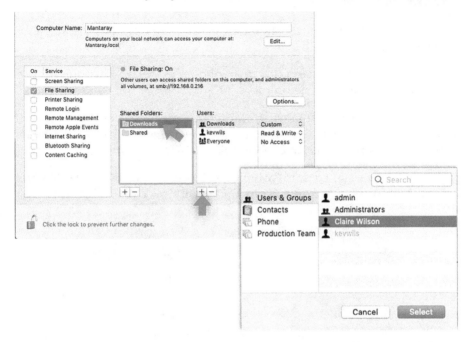

Select the users to whom you want to grant access. Under 'users' click the plus sign and select the name of the person you want to give access to your folder. Click 'select'. This will create a username and password you'll need to give the person so they can gain access to the folder.

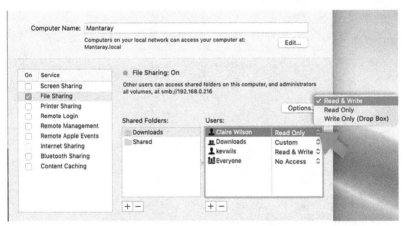

Next select what access you want to give them: read only or read & write. Click the selector next to the name to change this. If you want anyone to be able to access the folder, set 'everyone' to 'read & write' or 'read only'.

iCloud Drive

iCloud Drive is Apple's file hosting service for devices running iOS, MacOS, or Windows 7/8/10.

This feature allows users to save photos, videos, Keynote, Pages, Numbers files, and music online.

The idea being, you can start work on your mac and continue on your iPad/iPhone on the train, for example. Users get 5 GB of storage for free, but this space will be expandable via subscription.

Once you have signed into your iCloud account on Mac OS Mojave, you will find a new option in your finder window called 'iCloud Drive'.

If you haven't signed in you can do so by going to system preferences, clicking iCloud and entering your Apple ID username and password.

Follow the instructions on the dialog box and click next.

Here you can select what you want to sync between your mac and your iCloud drive. Eg, you can share photos in iPhoto, sync your contacts and email between devices, sync your calendar and notes all by ticking the boxes above.

To start using iCloud drive, you can save documents from any of the iWork Applications. For example, say you are working on a document in Pages, you can save it in the Pages section of iCloud drive as circled above.

Now if I want to carry on with my letter I can get my documents on my iPad/iPhone. You'll find them in your Files App, you will see same folders as on your mac.

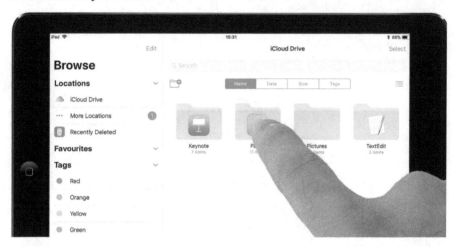

The document was saved in the Pages folder. If you tap in the pages folder you will find your saved document.

Tap on the file icon to open it up. Note, you'll need the same app on your iPad as you used on your Mac to edit the documents. In this example, I used Pages word processor installed on Mac and iPad. You can download the apps from the app store if you need them.

iCloud Drive File Sharing

Any file in iCloud Drive can now be shared with another person through a new link feature. The link option will give direct access to specific files and folders while keeping the rest of your iCloud Drive private.

Select how you want to share the link with the other person. In this example I'm going to send it via email. Click 'add people', to grant permission to a person to view your file.

Click 'mail', then adjust the options below. Set 'who can access' to anyone with a link. If you just want the person you're sharing with to see the file, leave this setting on its default.

Enter the person's email address, add a subject if you wish and a short message. Click 'send'.

When the other person checks their email, they can click on the link in the email to see your file.

If the other person is on a Windows machine, they can click the link to download.

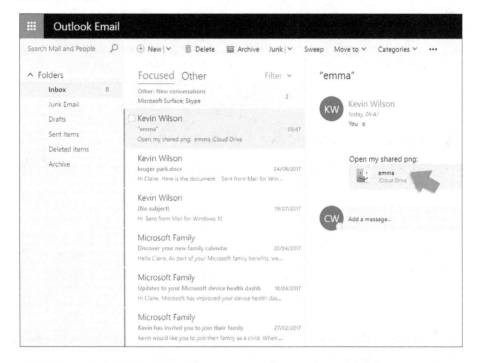

Click 'download' from the prompt.

Managing App Windows

When working on your Mac it's best to arrange the windows on your desktop, especially when you're using more than one application at a time. For example, you could be browsing the web and writing a document at the same time- perhaps you're researching something, you could have the Pages App open and your web browser next to it on the screen.

Moving a Window

To move a window, move your mouse pointer to the title bar at the top of the window.

Now click and drag the window to your desired position on the screen.

Release your mouse button. You can move the windows to anywhere on the desktop.

Resizing a Window

To resize a window, move your mouse pointer to the bottom right corner of the window - your pointer should turn into a double edged arrow.

The double edged arrow means you can resize the window. Now click and drag the edge of the window until it is the size you want.

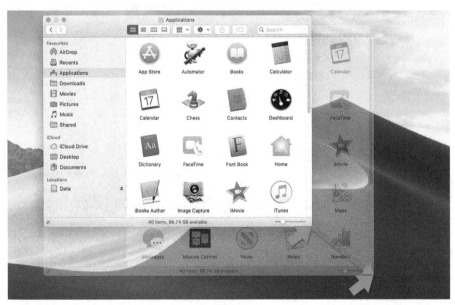

You can drag any edge of the window - left, bottom or right edge, but I find using the corner allows you to freely resize the window much more easily.

Minimise, Maximise & Close a Window

On the top left hand side of every window, you'll see three icons. These three icons appear on all apps that run in a window. Lets take a look at an example. Here's the Finder window.

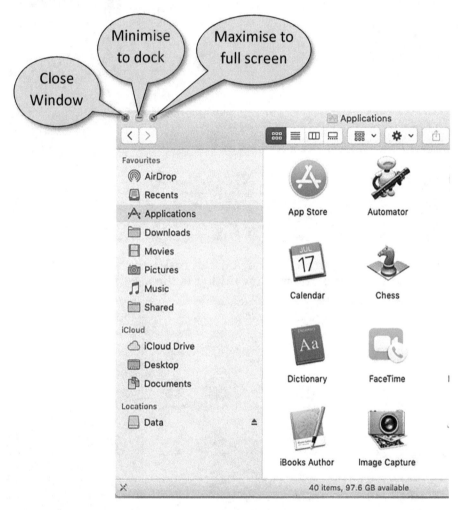

Use the first icon to close the window. Note that this doesn't close the app fully.

The second icon will minimise the window to the space on the right hand side of the dock.

The third icon will maximise the window so it fills the entire screen, or if the window is already maximised, using the same icon, restore the window to its original size.

Dashboard

A useful utility that contains "widgets" which are small applications designed to accomplish a single task, such as a calculator, dictionary, clock, translator, calendar etc.

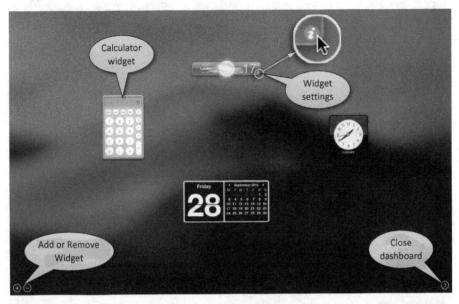

To change settings on a widget, hover your mouse over the widget and click the 'i' icon that appears on the bottom right.

To add a widget, click the '+' symbol on the bottom left of the screen.

To remove a widget, click the '-' icon on the bottom left. You'll see a small black 'x' appear on the top right of each widget. Click the 'x' on the widgets you want to remove.

Spotlight Search

Spotlight is a search engine that allows you to locate anything on your mac by typing it in.

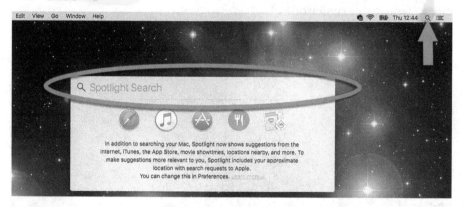

If you look in the top right hand corner of the screen, you'll see what looks like a magnifying glass. Click the icon and type in what you're searching for.

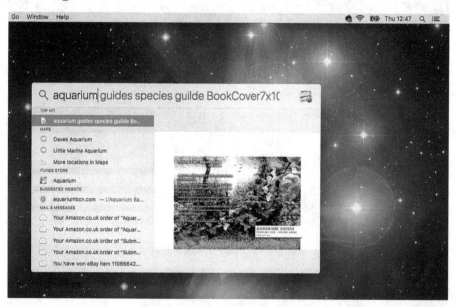

If you look down the left hand side of the window that appears, spotlight automatically sorts out the different types of files, such as documents, photographs, email messages and web searches into different sections to make it easier to find.

Spotlight can also give you definitions of words.

Notification Centre

Notification Centre shows a list of alerts from applications and displays notifications asking you to complete an associated action. As well as widgets for local weather, your calendar and reminders.

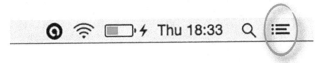

Notification centre is split into two tabs. The tab marked 'today' - shown below, gives you the current date, day, weather widget and your calendar at a glance.

You can see your appointments in your calendar widget, as you can see there is a reading event happening. As well as a reminder that there is a meeting the next day.

Chapter 3: Getting Around Your Mac

You can add more widgets by clicking 'edit' at the bottom of the screen. In the window that opens up, the list on the left hand side are the widgets you have added to your notification centre. The list on the right hand side are the ones available to add.

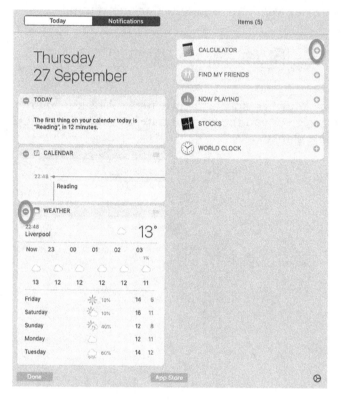

Just click the little green plus sign next to the widget you want to add. To remove any widgets just click the red minus sign next to the widget.

To download more notification center widgets, click 'app store' at the bottom of the window. In the app store, click the price or 'get' to download the widget, then 'install app'.

The second tab is your list of notifications, alerts and messages, such as new email, new tweets, new events, current iTunes tracks etc. There are three types of notifications: banners, alerts, and badges.

Banners

These are displayed for a short period in the upper right corner of the Mac's screen, and then slide off to the right.

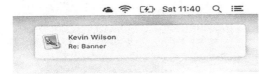

The application's icon is displayed on the left side of the banner, while the message from the application will be displayed on the right side.

Alerts

Same as banners, except an alert has a call to action on the right hand side and will not disappear from the screen until the user takes action.

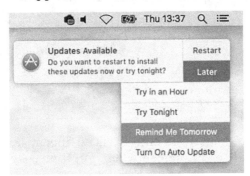

Badges

These are red notification icons that are displayed on the application's icon. They indicate the number of items available for the application.

83

You can change these settings by opening notification center and clicking on the settings icon on the bottom right of the window - shown below.

This allows you to set how the alerts and notifications appear on your screen when events happen.

For example email messages shown below appear in a banner on the top right hand side of the screen when a new message comes in.

It shows you the sender's name, subject and the first line of two of the message. To read the whole message click on the banner before it disappears.

Most of these settings you wont need to change.

Dynamic Desktop

Apple have introduced a new feature in Mojave called Dynamic Desktops, in which wallpapers shift according to the time of day, changing the lighting and look of the wallpaper during the course of the day.

In the afternoon, the wallpaper is at its brightest, and at night, the sky in the wallpaper shifts to darker blue to reflect the evening. This helps to adapt the screen look and brightness to the changing ambient light levels during the day.

To adjust your wallpapers, right click on the desktop and select 'change desktop background'.

At the top you'll see 'mojave' and 'dynamic' in the selection. This means the desktop will change during the course of the day. At the moment this is the only dynamic desktop, however more will be added soon.

85

Handoff

Handoff is a continuity feature that allows you to start something on one device such as your iPhone or iPad, then seamlessly pick up and continue on another such as your Mac.

First, you'll need to enable Handoff on your devices. To enable Handoff on your iPhone, open the settings app from your home screen. Tap 'General', then 'Handoff'. Tap the switch to set 'Handoff' to 'on'.

Now enable your Bluetooth. Go to the settings app, select 'Bluetooth'. Tap the switch to set it to 'on'.

To enable it on your Mac, go to the System Preferences in the Apple menu. Tap 'Bluetooth' and turn it on.

Go back to System Preferences and click 'General'. Click the check box next to "Allow Handoff between this Mac and your iCloud Devices".

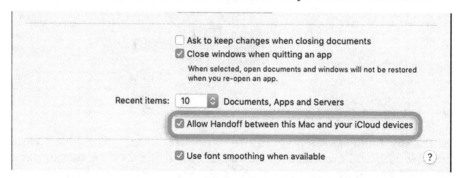

Now for this demo, I'm going to start typing an email message on my iPhone. When you bring your iPhone near your Mac, you'll see the icon of the app you're using, appear on the left hand side of the dock.

Click on this icon on the dock to continue using the app. In this demo, you'll see the email open up on your Mac.

Here, you'll be able to continue from where you left off.

Universal Clipboard

This is another interesting feature that allows you to cut, copy and paste with your clipboard across all your Apple Devices; iPhone, iPad as well as your Mac. This works when all your devices are logged in with your apple id.

In the demonstration below, I have copied a paragraph from a Pages document on the Macbook Pro, and pasted it into an email on my iPhone.

To do this, highlight the text from an application on your Mac, right click and click copy.

On your iPad or iPhone, go into the application you are going to paste the text into, tap and hold your finger in the position you want the text to appear, and tap paste from the menu that appears.

Universal Clipboard also works the other way around, if you wanted to copy some text from your phone and paste into a document on your Mac.

Instant HotSpot

Also known as tethering, Instant Hotspot allows you to share your iPhone's internet connection easily with your Mac. To set this up, on your iPhone go to the settings app and tap 'personal hotspot'. Toggle 'personal hotspot' to on, then enable your bluetooth.

On your Mac, your iPhone appears in the WiFi menu as another network.

In this example the iPhone is called 'Elluminet21', so I'd select that one from the WiFi networks.

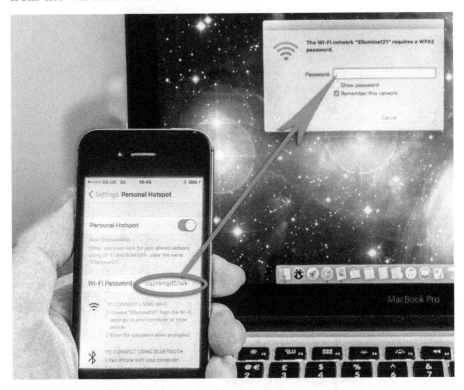

When prompted on your Mac, enter the WiFi password shown in the personal hotspot settings on your iPhone, as show above.

Using Siri

Siri has finally made it to the Mac and works pretty much as she does on the iPhone.

You can find Siri on your dock...

...and on the top right hand side of your screen.

So whenever you need Siri, just click the icon on the top right of the screen, or the icon on the Dock. Tap the mic icon, circled below...

...and ask Siri whatever you need.

It's as simple as that.

Apple Pay

Apple Pay is available on the Mac and you can use it to purchase items from participating stores using Safari. You'll also need an iPhone or Apple Watch with Apple Pay set up.

Setup

To set up Apple Pay, go to the settings app on your iPhone, scroll down and tap 'wallet & apple pay'. Then tap 'add card'.

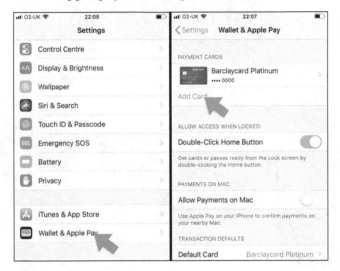

If you already have a credit/debit card registered with your Apple ID, then apple pay will ask you to add this one.

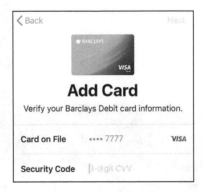

If this is the card you want to use, then enter the 3 digit security code and tap 'next' on the top right. Hit 'agree' on the terms and conditions. Your card will be added.

If you want to add a different card, tap 'add a different card' underneath.

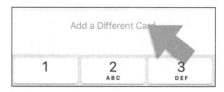

Position the card so it fills the white rectangle on your screen. Apple Pay will scan your card and automatically enter your details

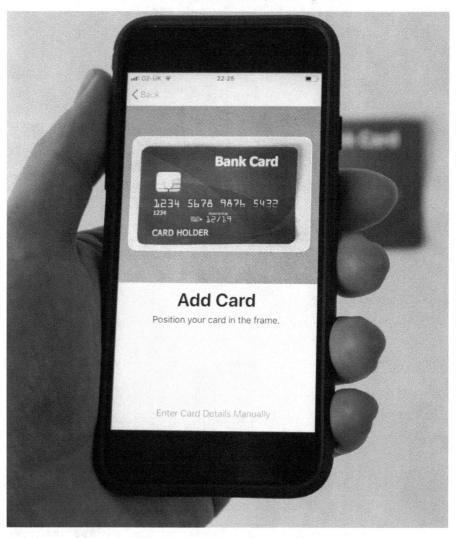

If you can't get the camera to scan the card, tap 'enter card details manually' then key in your card number, exp dates, and so on.

Tap next. Check and confirm your card details. Make any changes if necessary, so the details match those on your card. Tap next, then tap 'agree' to the terms and conditions.

Now you'll need to verify your card. Some banks use different methods, so read the instructions on the screen. In this example, the bank will send a code via SMS to the phone number registered when the bank account was opened. Tap 'next'.

Check your SMS messages and enter the verification code in the field. Tap 'next'.

93

Using Apple Pay on your Mac

To be able to use Apple Pay on your Mac, you will need to use the Safari Web Browser and have an Apple device such as your iPhone near by. On participating websites, you will see "pay with Apple Pay Button". When you click on this button, you will see an authentication prompt on your nearby iPhone or Apple Watch. This uses the continuity feature.

Browse your favourite shopping site and, when you're ready to buy, click on the Apple Pay button.

Once you click the Apple Pay button on the website, a notification will pop up on your iPhone asking you to authorise the transaction. You can do this by using Touch ID on your iPhone.

You'll only see the Apple Pay logos on participating websites and only if you have your iPhone set up and in the vicinity of your Mac.

Auto Unlock

You can now automatically unlock your Mac using another Apple Device such as Apple Watch.

Open your Macbook's lid or tap a key while wearing your Apple Watch to unlock your Mac from sleep mode.

Auto Unlock only works when waking your Mac from sleep. If you restart your Mac or start it up from Shut Down, then you will need to enter a password to unlock.

First you need to enable 'two factor authentication'. To do this, open your web browser and head over to...

```
appleid.apple.com
```

...and enter your Apple ID and password.

Click 'edit' under the security section, then 'get started' under 2 step authentication and follow the on screen prompts.

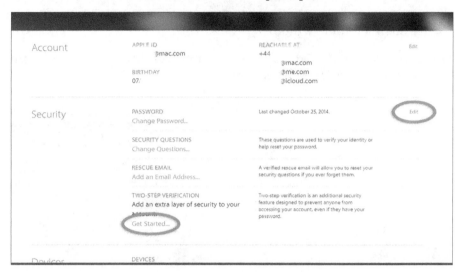

Now, go to system preferences, click security and in the general tab, click 'allow your apple watch to unlock your mac'.

Enter mac password.

Now once it is set up, you can wake and unlock your Mac simply by opening up the lid, or tapping a key while wearing your watch.

The Mac Keyboard

The Mac keyboard is not much different from a standard computer keyboard, although there are a few keys to take note of. These are highlighted below.

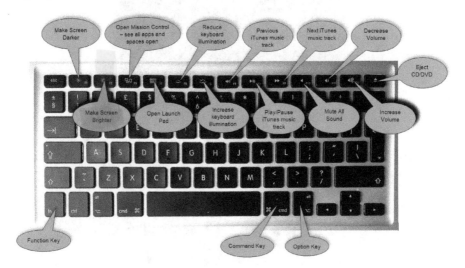

The fn (function key) is useful when you need to access a second option on the function keys along the top of the keyboard.

The cmd (command key) is useful for keyboard shortcuts eg copy and paste (Command C & Command V)

Hold down command key, then tap the letter corresponding to the command you want to execute.

Useful Keyboard Shortcuts

Use the command key on your keyboard to execute these commands.

Using the command key, you can execute several commands common to most applications

$$\mathcal{H} + P = \text{Print}$$

Q = Quit

X = Cut   W = Close Window

Z = Undo   C = Copy

A = Select All   S = Save

H = Hide   V = Paste

F = Find   O = Open Window

G = Find Next   E = Eject

M = Minimize   N = New

- = Zoom Out   + = Zoom In

If you're having some trouble with an application, you can force it to quit using the combo: command option escape

Select the application from the popup window and click 'force quit'.

MacOS Startup Keys

When your Mac starts up, you can hit certain keys to use different tools. This is particularly useful if your Mac encounters problems or you want to re-install MacOS - eg, hold down option key to select boot device.

When your Mac restarts, quickly hold down the keyboard combo until you see the Apple logo.

Keyboard Combo	Command
Shift ⇧	Start up in safe mode with minimal drivers.
Option ⌥	Open start up manager. Allows you to select boot device.
C	Start up from a bootable CD, DVD, or USB thumb drive
D	Run Apple Hardware Test.
Option D	Run Apple Hardware Test over the Internet.
Option N	Start up from a NetBoot server using an image stored on MacOS Server.
Command R	Start up in Recovery Mode using local recovery partition.
Command Option R	Start up in Recovery Mode using recovery data from Apple's Servers.
Command Option P R	Reset NVRAM. Hold keys until you hear startup sound.
T	Start up in target disk mode, allows your mac to be used as if it was an external hard drive.

Use both the shift, command and option keys to execute these commands.

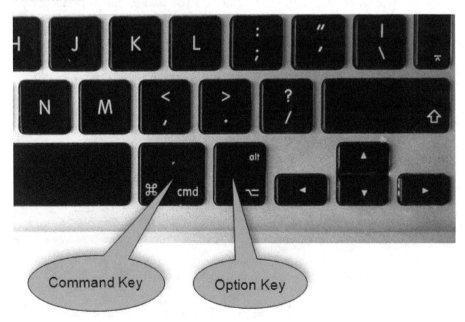

Making Gestures

If you have a Macbook with a trackpad, you can use a number of finger gestures to operate certain features of MacOS.

One Finger Point and Tap

You can move your mouse pointer across the screen by using one finger on the trackpad. Tap your finger on the pad to select an icon and is the equivalent of your left mouse click.

Two Finger Scroll

You can scroll down web pages and documents using two fingers on the track pad.

Two Finger Rotate

You can rotate things on the screen by using your forefinger and thumb on the trackpad making a twisting action with your wrist. This works well when viewing photographs or browsing a map.

Two Finger Swipe

Swiping two fingers across the trackpad swipes between pages in a document, book or on a website.

Four Finger Open Launchpad

Use your thumb and three fingers on the trackpad and draw your fingers and thumb together will open Launchpad where you can select an app to open.

Magic Mouse

A Bluetooth wireless mouse with multi gesture support. We'll take a look at these gestures below.

Left Click

Primary select button to click or double click on an icon

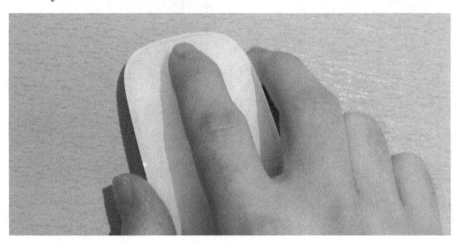

Right Click

Secondary click or right mouse button click to reveal context menus.

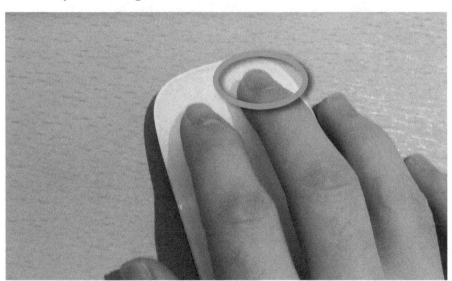

Scrolling

Scroll vertically or horizontally around a page, image, document, etc. Run your finger over the surface of the mouse - up and down, left and right to scroll pages

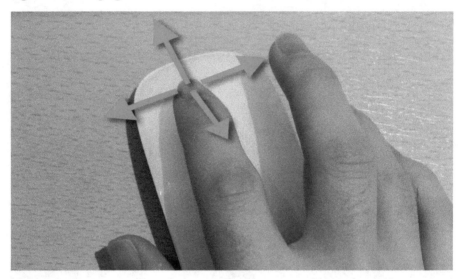

Swipe

Use two fingers to swipe left and right across the surface of the mouse to move a page forward or backward when reading a document or website.

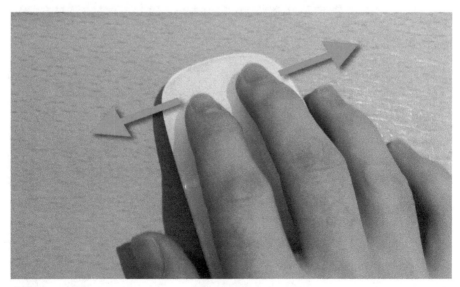

Find your Mouse Pointer

If you have lost your mouse pointer somewhere on the screen you can wiggle your finger backwards and forwards across your track-pad .

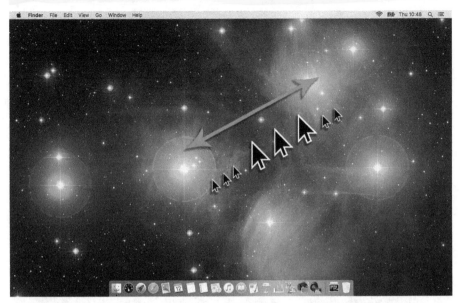

Wiggle your mouse and your cursor will grow to a larger size making it easier to find.

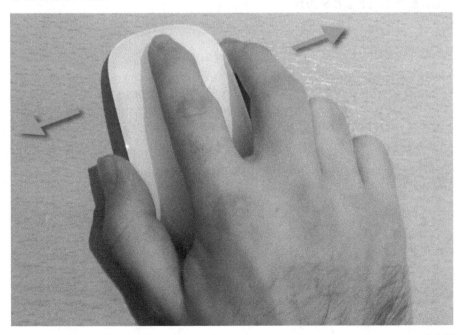

The Touch Bar

On the newer Macbooks, you'll find another navigation bar along the top of your keyboard. This is called the Touch Bar.

Touch Bar Layout

On the Touch Bar, you can tap icons and swipe through lists to aid your navigation on screen.

Icons on the 'application strip' of the Touch Bar change depending on the app you're using. For example, if you're using the photo app, you'll find icons to crop or rotate an image or scroll through your photos. For the mail app, you'll find icons for replying to or deleting emails. In maps app, you'll find icons to rotate or zoom into a map.

The Touch Bar is broken down into the following general layout.

System Button: Cancel, done, escape, etc

Application Strip: icons for currently active app

Control Strip: screen brightness, volume, siri etc

Control Strip

Click on the desktop and you'll see these icons on the touch bar. On the right hand side, you'll see the control strip. Tap the left arrow to expand the strip to reveal all the icons.

Once you expand the bar to show all the icons. This is where you'll find your icons to increase/decrease screen brightness, desktop spaces, launchpad, increase/decrease keyboard illumination brightness, skip previous track, play pause, skip next track, mute volume, decrease/increase volume, and ask siri.

Tap the x on the left hand side to close the control strip.

Application Strip

The application strip is the middle section of the touch bar where you can control common actions in various Mac Apps such as Safari, Mail, Photos and so on. So for example, if you open Safari web browser, the application strip will look like this.

You'll see icons for all your most recently visited websites. Swipe left and right over the Touch Bar to see all the icons. Tap on an icon to open the corresponding website.

Once you've navigated to a website, the Touch Bar icons will change again.

Tap on 'search or enter website name' to do a Google Search or enter a website address in Safari, then type into the search field on the screen.

You can also use the Touch Bar with other Apps. For example if you open the Mail App the Touch Bar shows your common task toolbar.

If you compose or reply to a message, the Touch Bar changes to show your formatting tools. Tap on any of the icons with your finger.

Try the Photos App, when you open the app, the Touch Bar shows.

You can slide your finger across the thumbnail navigation on the center of the Touch Bar to scroll through your photos.

You'll find that the Touch Bar will change according to the app that is currently running. Note that not all apps support this feature.

Customise Touch Bar

You can tweak the Touch Bar to your own preferences. To do this, open the app you want to customise, eg Finder. From the drop down menu, select 'Customise Touch Bar'.

Now from the touch icon selections on your screen, click and drag the icon you want to the touch bar.

You can also tap and drag the icons to reorder them or move them.

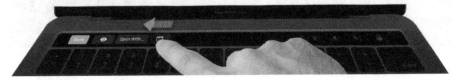

To remove an icon, drag it off the Touch Bar.

Click 'done' on the top left of the icon selection pane when you're finished.

Dark Mode

Dark mode allows you to change the look of the interface to tackle the problem of eye strain when using a computer in low light conditions or for long periods of time.

To enable dark mode, open your system preferences and select 'general'. Change the 'appearance' option to 'dark'.

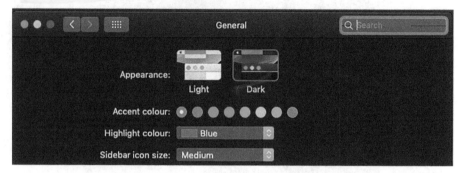

Dark Mode is designed to put less strain on the eyes and is intended to make reading a computer screen easier.

Here you can see the interface has a high contrast visual look with dark backgrounds and white text.

The dock along the bottom also shows up in dark grey showing up the icons a lot clearer.

Find my Mac

This feature allows you to pinpoint your Mac's location and is quite useful if you have misplaced your Mac or had it stolen.

Setup

First you need to activate it on your Mac. To do this, open the system preferences app and click "iCloud".

Scroll down to 'find my Mac'

Also make sure location services is turned on. To do this go back to the settings home page and select 'security & privacy'. Select the 'privacy' tab. Click the small padlock on the bottom left of the window and enter your username and password. Then click 'enable location services'.

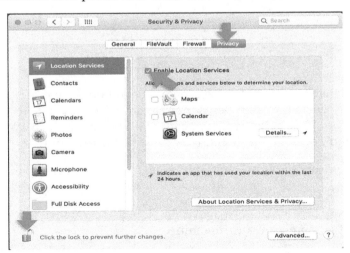

Locating & Taking Action

On any device - iPad, Mac or PC, open your web browser and navigate to:

`www.icloud.com`

Sign in with your Apple ID. Select 'find iPhone' from the iCloud control panel.

You can locate all your Apple devices. Select the name of your device from the drop down menu in the top middle of the screen.

You'll see a green dot appear on the map. This is the current location of your device.

On the right hand side of the screen, you can take action. Here you can click 'play sound' to play an annoying sound on your mac wherever it might be. This helps you to locate it if you've lost it in your house somewhere, or annoy a thief if they have possession of it.

You can also remotely lock your mac to prevent any unauthorised access.

Finally you can erase your mac completely. To remove any personal data that is stored on your machine.

Pairing Bluetooth Devices

You can pair bluetooth keyboards, headphones, and most bluetooth capable devices.

To pair a device, first put the device into pairing mode. You'll need to refer to the device's instructions to find specific details on how to do this. On most devices, press and hold the pairing button until the status light starts flashing. This means the device is ready to be paired with your iPhone.

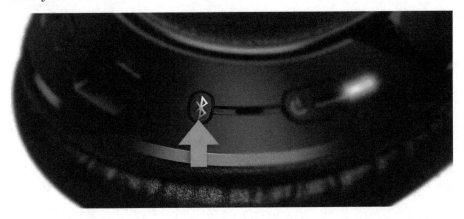

On your Mac, open the system preferences app. From the app, select 'bluetooth'. On the left hand side of the window click 'turn bluetooth on', if it isn't already.

The bluetooth device will appear in the list. Click 'connect'.

Chapter 4

Using Applications

MacOS Mojave comes with a good number of Applications pre-installed, from Maps to Photographs to Word Processors to Internet and email.

There are a wide variety of Applications or Apps available for the Mac that can be purchased and downloaded from the App Store.

Applications on Mojave can be found in a number of different places. Finder/Applications, the Dock or Launch Pad.

The easiest place to find them is on Launch Pad and the Dock.

Lets take a closer look.

Launching Your Applications

You can find applications on the dock at the bottom of your screen.

You can also find apps by hitting the Launch Pad icon on the dock.

If there are apps you use a lot, you can drag them from launch pad to the dock.

The next time you need the application just click on the icon on the dock.

Chapter 4: Using Applications

You can also launch applications from the 'applications' folder in your finder window.

If the application you launched is one you use quite often, but is not permanently on the dock, you can easily add it.

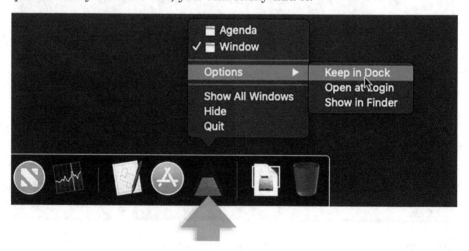

This will keep the application's icon in the dock whether it is running or not.

Killing Unresponsive Apps

Sometimes apps lock up and freeze and there is no way to close the app using conventional means.

Press **CMD - OPTION - ESC**, as shown below...

From the popup window, select the app you want to shut down, then click 'force quit'.

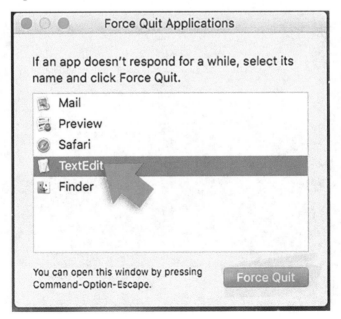

App Store

The App Store has been totally rebuilt and has a new interface. You'll find the icon on your launchpad or dock.

You can also access the app store from the apple menu on the very top left of the screen.

Once you launch app store, you'll see the main screen. Here you can type in the name of the app you are looking for in the search field on the top left of the screen, or click the 'categories' icon to browse categories such as reference, productivity and entertainment listed down the panel on the left hand side.

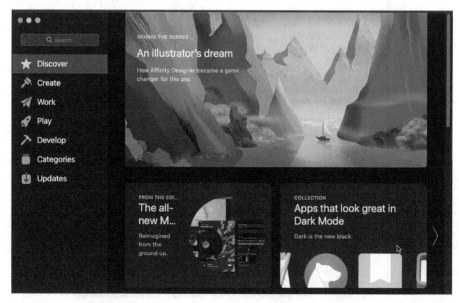

To buy or download anything, just click the price - or click 'get' if it's free.

The buttons will change to 'buy app', or 'install' if it's free. Click on the icon again to confirm the download.

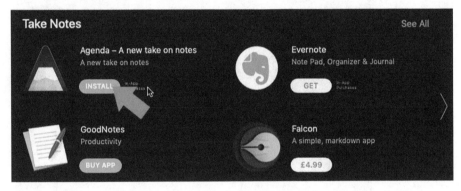

Sign in with your Apple ID email and password if prompted.

The app will download. Once the download and install is complete, you will find your new app in Launchpad on your dock.

You can also find your new app in the applications folder in Finder.

Tabbed Apps

Tabbed Apps gives you the ability to open multiple application windows in tabs in the same window rather than multiple windows. You can switch between these by clicking on the tabs, circled below.

If your windows don't automatically open as tabs, you can merge all your windows using the 'merge all windows' command. You can find this on the 'window' menu at the top of your screen.

This will merge all the open windows of the same application into one tabbed window.

Maps

Another great feature in MacOS Mojave is the maps app. You'll find the maps app icon either on your dock or on launchpad.

With the Maps app, you can explore cities, places of interest, as well as finding directions to a particular destination.

Getting Directions

You can type the name of the city or venue you are looking for in the search field at top centre of the screen. You can also enter postal/zip codes to find specific areas.

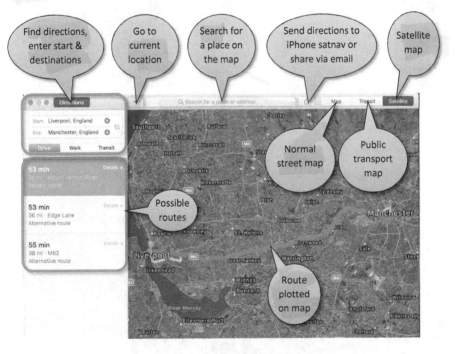

Click 'directions' on the top left of the screen. Type in your location and your destination in to the fields shown, and maps will come back with a route plus turn-by-turn directions for you to print or sent to your iPhone SatNav/GPS.

Chapter 4: Using Applications

To send the map to your iPhone or iPad, click the share icon, then from the drop down menu, select your device.

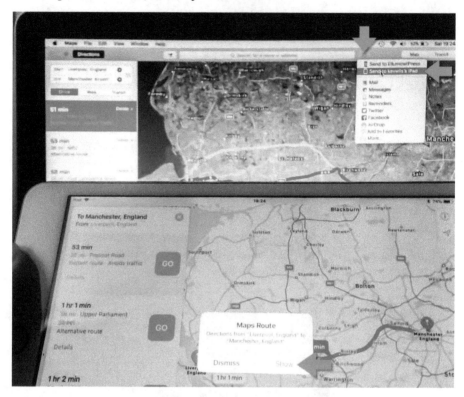

On your device, you'll see a prompt. Tap 'show' and the route will appear on your device.

If you're using an iPhone, tap on 'go' next to the preferred route on the left hand side and you can use your phone as a GPS/SatNav.

You can also use the share icon to send the map to someone over email, iMessage, post it on facebook and so on. Just select the option from the menu.

Explore in 3D

Using the satellite map, you can also view cities in 3D. Type the name of the city into the search field on the top middle of the screen. Select 'satellite' from the map selections on the top right.

Click '3D' on the bottom right hand side. Use the '+' & '-' icons on the bottom right to zoom in and out of your map. Click and drag your mouse to move the map around the screen.

Click 'show' on the bottom left of the screen. Here you can show weather, air quality, traffic, and street/building labels.

Apple have started adding indoor features to their maps app. This includes interior layouts and maps of airports, shopping malls and other venues.

Apple Books

Formerly known as iBooks, Apple Books allows you to download and read ebooks.

To open Apple Books on your mac, click the Apple Books icon on your dock.

Hit 'get started' and go to Book Store. Once opened, you'll see all the books you have purchased or downloaded. This is your book library.

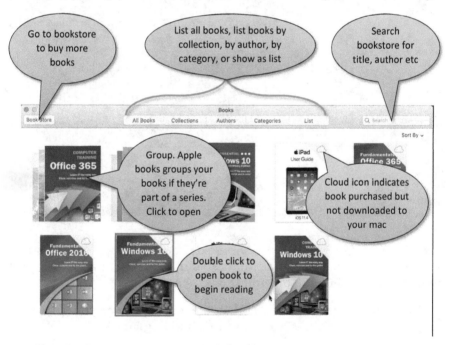

Double click on the book covers to open the books.

Tap on the cloud icons on the top left of the book cover thumbnails to download the book to your mac.

Once the books are open, you can 'turn the pages' by swiping two fingers left or right across the trackpad on your macbook. If you are using a mouse, click the left or right edges of the screen to turn the page.

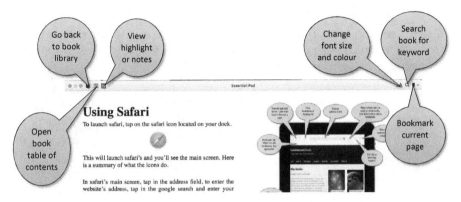

You can also add notes and highlight parts of the book. Click and drag your mouse across the text you want to highlight, then right click on the selection.

Two menus to take note of. The first ~~~~~~~~~~~~~~~~d side of the screen and allows you ⬤ ⬤ ⬤ ⬤ ⬤ a r bookmarked sites. You can tap on ar ☐ Add Note o return to the sites.

🗑 Remove Highlight

Copy

More ▶

From the popup menu select a colour to highlight the text.

To add a note, click 'add note' then type your note into the post-it that appears. To see all your notes click 'view highlight or notes' icon on the tool bar at the top.

Two menus to take note of. The first menu is on This is the part of safari side of the screen and allows you to access you want to keep your bookmarked sites. You can tap on any of these eye on... return to the sites.

Chapter 4: Using Applications

To buy or download more books, click 'Book Store' on the top left hand side of the screen.

You can search for a particular book by typing author or title into the search field on the top right of the screen. Alternatively, you can search through the categories on the top bar.

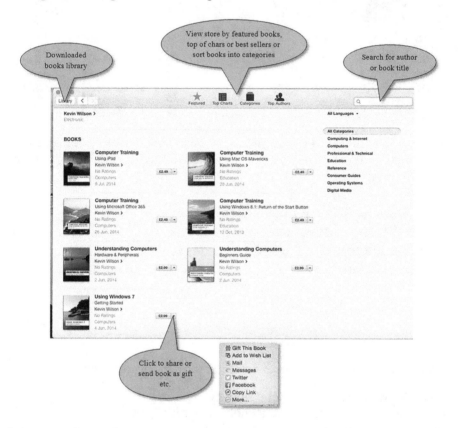

Once you have found a book you want, click the price, this will download it and add it to your bookshelf in your library.

Click on the book cover to see more details about the book such as sample pages, technical stats, reviews and write ups.

You can find all your books that you have purchased, by clicking the library button on the top left of the screen.

All your books are synchronized across all your apple devices; iPhone, iPad and iBooks on your Mac.

Notes

You'll find the note app on your dock or launchpad.

When you open the notes app, you'll see the main screen. Here you can see your notes you have created either on your iPad/iPhone or on your Mac - these are listed in the centre pane.

On the right hand pane, you'll be able to edit a note you've selected in the centre pane.

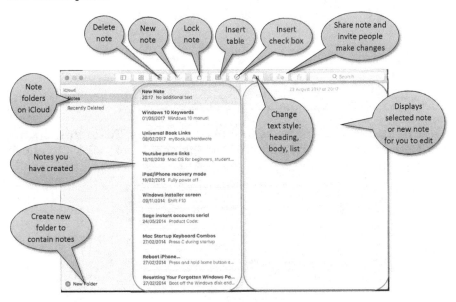

Click on a note in the list to view. Click the 'new note' icon to create a new note.

There's an option to pin your most used notes to the top of the notes app for quick access to lists and other frequently used notes.

To do this, right click on the note in the list and from the popup menu, click 'pin note'. This will make sure it stays at the top of the list.

Tables can also be added to individual notes for better organization. Open an existing note or create a new one. Click on the 'insert table icon' on the toolbar.

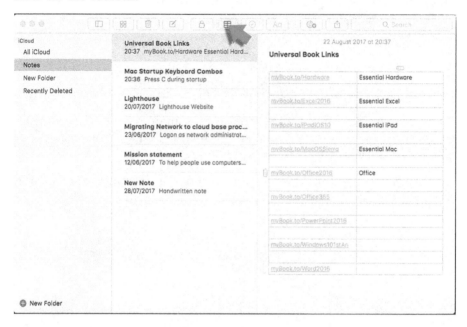

You can also add check boxes to make 'to do' lists. To do this, open a new note or select one to edit. To add the check box, click the check box icon on the toolbar.

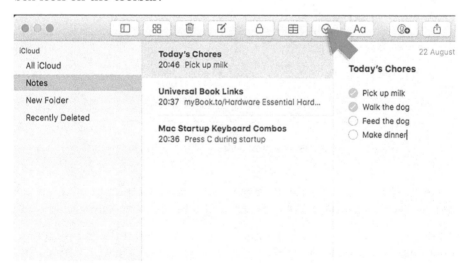

Once you have completed the task, click the circle next to it, to mark the task as complete.

iCal Calendar

This utility is useful for storing all your friends email addresses, phone numbers, etc. These can be synced with your iPad, iPod touch or and iPhone. I find it easiest to view the calendar in month view as shown below.

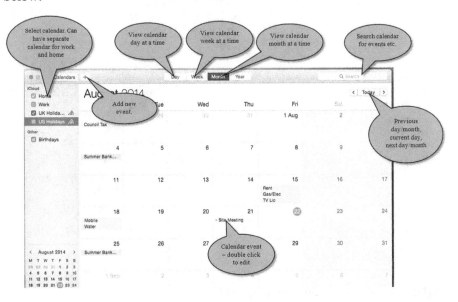

Adding an Event

The quickest way to add a new event is to click on the plus sign shown below, and enter the event name, time and day/date. iCal will then interpret this and add an appointment to your calendar.

As you can see iCal has interpreted the event and added an entry into your calendar. You can now add a location by typing it in

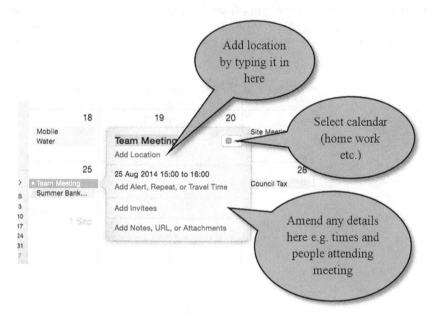

Add an Event from Email

Apple Mail scans your emails for possible events, meaning in some emails informing you of or inviting you to events, you'll see an option to add the event to your calendar. To add to your calendar, tap 'add' circled below/top-right.

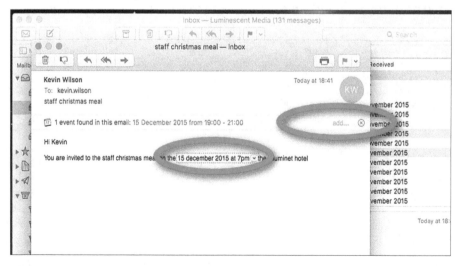

A window will appear detailing the event.

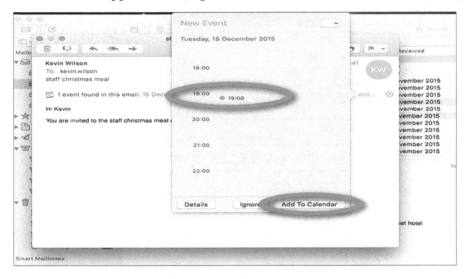

Click 'add to calendar' to add event.

Subscribing to Public Calendar

To add a public calendar go to the file menu and select 'new calendar subscription'.

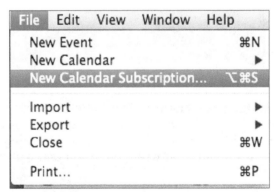

Then give it an appropriate name and enter the address as shown above. Some sample addresses are below. These are public holidays. The first is public holidays in the UK, the second public holidays in the US.

```
webcal://ical.mac.com/ical/UK32Holidays.ics
```

```
webcal://ical.mac.com/ical/US32Holidays.ics
```

Sharing Calendars & Creating Public Calendars

You can share calendars with friends, family and colleagues. This is useful if you have events or appointments that people in a team or group need to know about.

To share a calendar, right click on the calendar in the sidebar you want to share. From the pop up menu, select 'share calendar'.

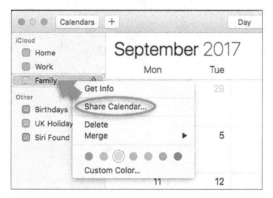

Select the people you want to share your calendar with. Start typing the person's name, then select the contact from the suggestions that appear. Do this with all the names you want to add.

If you want to make the calendar public, that is anyone with a link can view it, click the check box next to 'public calendar'. You'll see a URL appear. This is the link people will use to view the calendar. Click the icon next to the link to share it with people via email or social media.

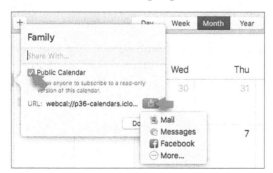

Image Capture

Image capture is useful for importing images from scanners and some cameras. You can find the image capture app in finder/applications and on your launchpad.

Down the left hand side of the window you will see a list of your installed devices; cameras and scanners.

Click on the device name to select it. On the right hand side you will see some information about the device.

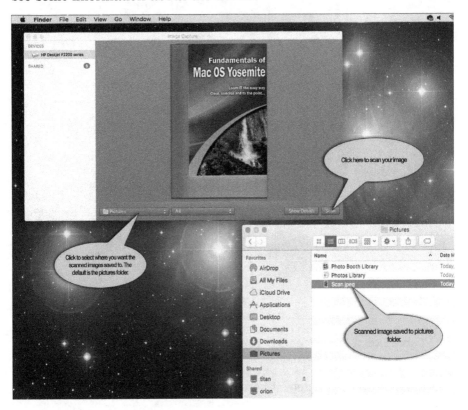

In this case the device connected is a scanner, so you will see an option to scan a document or image, preview it and save it to your pictures folder.

Photobooth

This is probably the most entertaining app that comes pre-installed on a Mac. I had the kids entertained for hours. You can find photobooth on your launch pad.

Photobooth allows you to use your Mac's on-board camera to make face distorting images; pull a funny face or key out the background and find yourself underwater, on the moon, or a roller coaster.

You can take a photo using your iSight camera by clicking on the camera icon in the centre.

You can also record video, if you select the film strip icon on the left hand side.

The fun part is when you get to the effects. Click 'effects' on the right hand side of the screen.

Have a look at the different effects below in the 9x9 grid. You can move around in the frame, or pull a funny face.

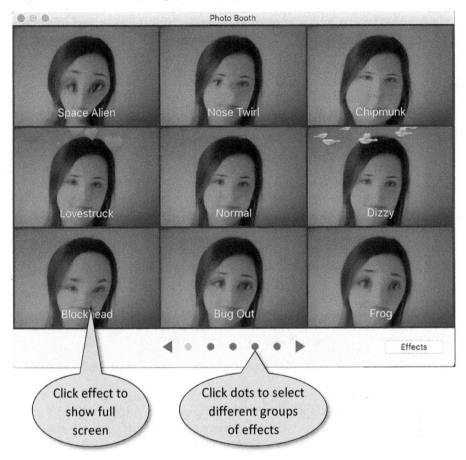

You can select different types of effects, from the distorted mirrors, shown above, to highlight effects or keyed backgrounds.

To do this, click on the dots along the bottom of the window, highlighted above, to browse through the different effects.

Have fun.

DVDs & Blu-rays

MacOS still has the ability to play DVDs but has a lack of support for blu-ray discs. Many of the new Macs no longer have built in DVD drives so you'll need to buy an external USB DVD or Blu-ray drive.

To play a Blu-ray, you'll also need to buy a piece of software called *Aiseesoft - Blu-ray Player*. You'll be able to download it from this website:

www.aiseesoft.com/blu-ray-player

Plug the drive into a spare USB port and insert the disc.

To watch a Blu-ray, open Aiseesoft Blu-ray player from launchpad.

To watch a DVD open DVD player. If you're using Mojave or later, DVD player no longer appears on launchpad or the applications folder. To open DVD player, if it doesn't open automatically, click spotlight search on the top right of the screen. Then type:

dvd player

From the spotlight search results 'top hits', click 'dvd player'.

Once DVD player has started, your DVD will begin and will usually go to the DVD menu.

Lets take a look at the control panel at the bottom of the movie window.

Select the play movie option on your DVD menu to begin your movie.

Press **ctrl - cmd - F** on your keyboard to view in full screen mode. Press they key combo again to exit full screen mode.

To skip chapters in full screen mode, move your mouse pointer and you'll see a control bar appear on the bottom.

Here, you can also return to the menu, adjust volume, skip/play/ pause or stop movie.

Voice Memos

You can record audio using your Mac's built in mic or a bluetooth external mic. You can record voice memos, meetings, and lectures.

You'll find the voice memo app on your launch pad.

Lets take a look at the main screen. Here you can see your previous recordings listed down the left hand side. Any recording you select here will appear in the white panel on the right hand side of the screen.

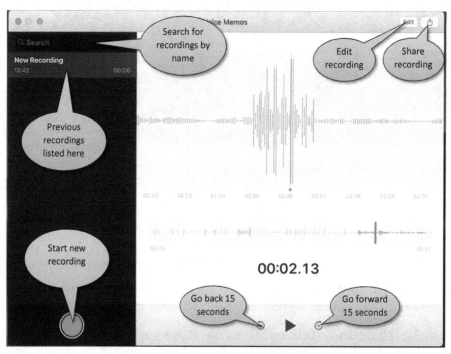

Click the play button in the grey panel on the right to playback the recording.

Recording Memos

To record a memo, simply click the red record button on the bottom left of the screen.

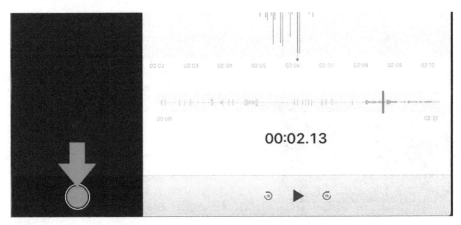

The memo app will start recording. You'll see a wave form appear in the middle of the screen to indicate the app is picking up audio.

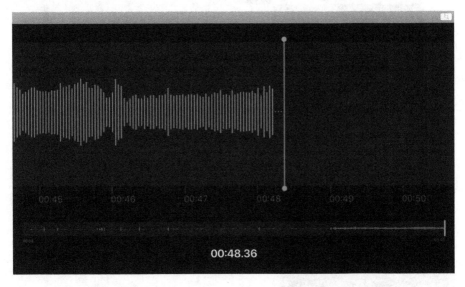

To pause a recording temporarily, click the pause icon on the left. To stop the recording, Click 'done'.

Your memo will appear in the list on the left hand side of the main screen.

139

Renaming Memos

The first thing you should do with a new voice memo recording is give it a meaningful name. The last thing you want is every memo called 'new recording.

To demonstrate this, we'll rename the voice memo we just recorded. Select the voice memo from the list on the left hand side.

From the file menu, select 'rename'.

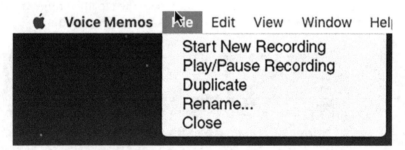

Delete the default text, then type in a meaningful name for the recording. Hit enter on the on screen keyboard to confirm the name.

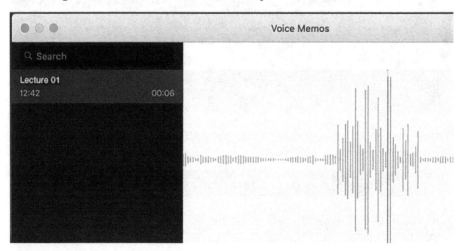

Trim a Memo

You can trim the beginning and the ends of the memo voice recording. To do this, select the recording you want to trim from the list on the left hand side of the main screen. Then click edit on the top right of the grey panel on the right hand side.

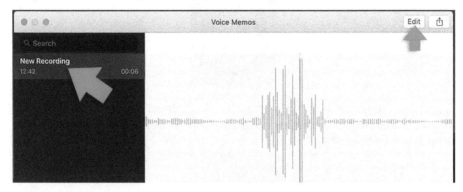

Click the trim icon on the top right

Now to trim the beginning and ends of the clip, drag the yellow handles along the track until you get to the start and end points you want.

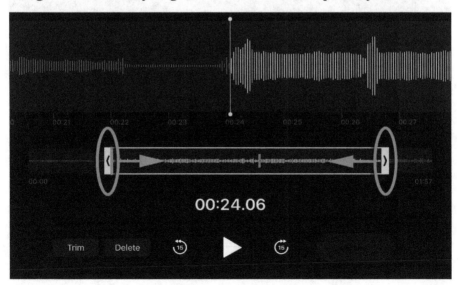

Click 'trim' when you're done.

News

The news app collects breaking stories from around the world and locally into one app, based on the topics you are interested in.

When you first start the app, you'll see a list of top stories, trending stories, and stories recommended for you. Scroll down the page, click on a story to read the details.

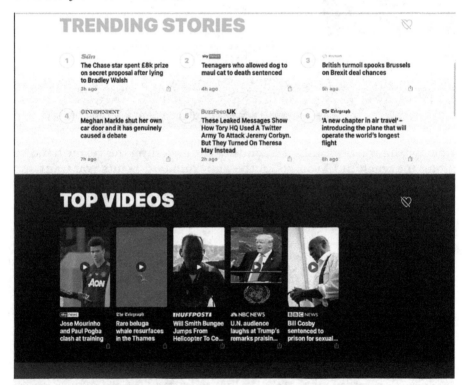

To open the side panel, tap the icon on the top left of the screen

From here you can select different news sources, magazines, newspapers and websites.

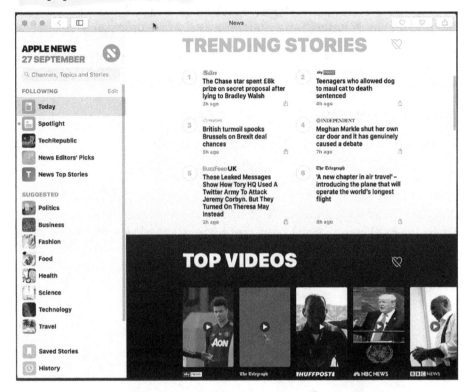

You can also search for specific channels. To do this, enter your search into the search field on the top left of the side panel.

Pages App

iWork (Apple Productivity Apps), is an office suite of applications that include Pages is a desktop publishing and word-processing package

If you don't have these applications on your Mac, you can download them from the App Store.

Starting Pages

To launch Pages, click the icon on your Launchpad

Once Pages 6 has opened, you can open a saved document, or click 'new document' to open a new one

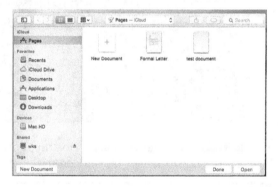

You will now need to select a template.

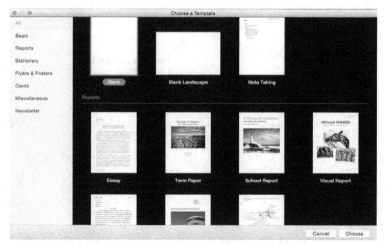

Once you have selected the template to use you will see the main work screen.

Let's take a closer look at the main editing screen.

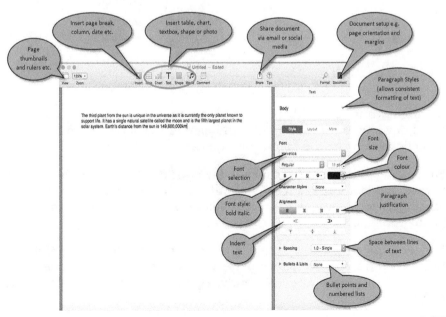

Formatting Text

To use Pages, begin typing in your text into the main window as shown below.

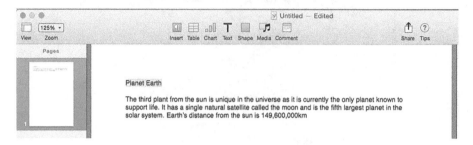

The text we entered before needs a heading. To add a heading type it in above the block of text.

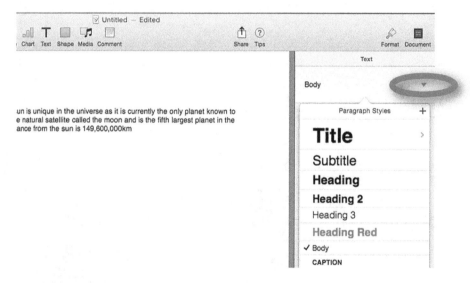

Highlight your text with the mouse as shown above then click the small down arrow on the right hand side of the screen (circled above) and click title from the menu that appears.

Formatting your document means laying it out in a style that is easy to read and looks attractive. This could involve changing fonts, making text bigger for headings, changing colour of text, adding graphics and photographs, etc.

For each document template you choose from the Template Chooser there are a number of pre-set paragraph styles. These are to help you format your document consistently, eg so all headings are the same font, size and colour.

146

Adding a Picture

The easiest way to add a picture is to find it in your finder window

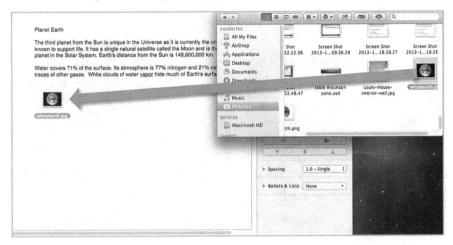

Then click and drag it into your document. It might be helpful to position your finder window next to your document window as shown in the figure above.

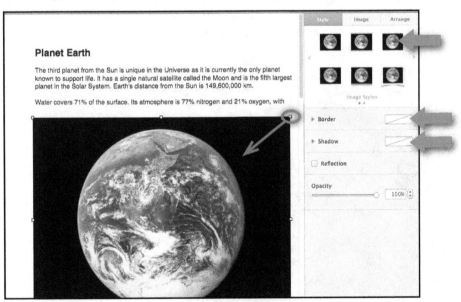

You can resize your image by clicking the resize handles, circled above, and dragging them. You can change the styles by adding borders and shadows by experimenting with the options in the style tab on the right hand side of the screen.

Instant Alpha

To get rid of these you use instant alpha from the format menu.

Click in the black area around the image. This is the bit we want to get rid of.

To remove any similar colours that are not initially deleted. On the image click your mouse on the black area of the image and drag it slightly until all the black changes colour as shown below.

Saving

You can either save your work on your iCloud Drive or your local documents on your mac.

Go to the file menu and select save...

Down the left hand side of the screen you will see some destinations where you can save your file. Take note of Documents under favourites - this is on your mac. Also take note of iCloud at the top, this saves onto your iCloud Drive.

The advantage of saving to your iCloud Drive is you can access and edit the documents you have just been working on, on your iPhone or iPad. Or even another mac.

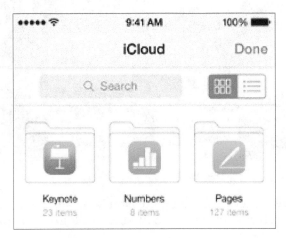

Keynote App

Keynote allows you to create multimedia presentations. To launch keynote, go to launch pad and click keynote.

Once keynote has loaded, you can select a saved file to open.

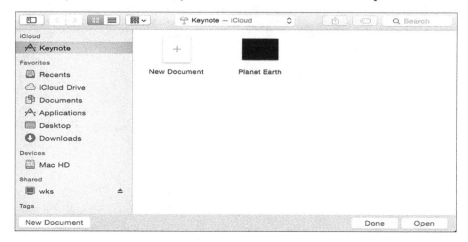

If you want to create a new presentation, click 'new document' on the bottom left hand side of the window. From here you can select from a variety of pre-designed templates with different themes, fonts and colours.

Once you have selected a template you will see the main screen as shown below. This is where you can start building your presentation.

Editing a Slide

Double click in the heading field shown above and enter a heading eg 'Planet Earth'. You can click and drag the heading wherever you like.

Adding a New Slide

Click the new slide button located on the bottom left of the screen

Click a slide layout from the options that appear.

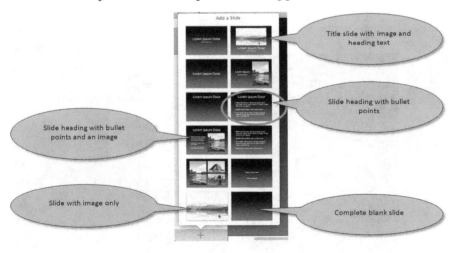

Add some text by double clicking on the text box that appears in the slide

Adding Media

The easiest way to add images and media to your slides is to find them in your finder window then drag and drop them onto the slides where the image is to appear.

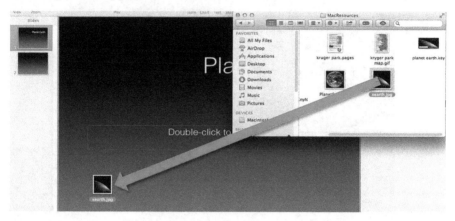

Browse through, to select the one you want, drag and drop the image to the slide.

If you want photographs, they can be dragged and dropped from your iPhoto library by starting up iPhoto finding the photograph in your library then dragging and dropping it onto your slide.

It helps to drag your iPhoto window over as shown above so you can see your slide underneath

Animations

Animations allow you to make objects such as text or photographs appear...

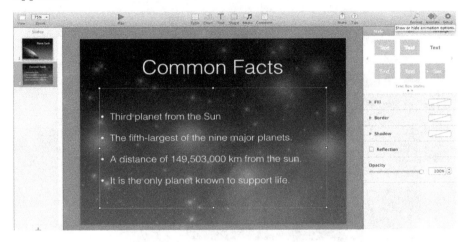

Click on your text box and select the animate icon located on the top right corner of your screen

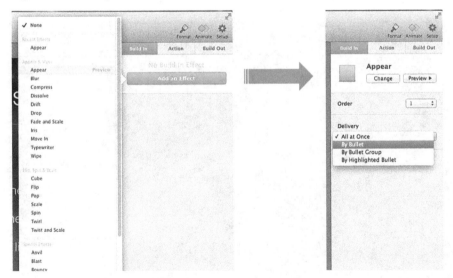

Then select an effect from the effects drop down menu (shown above left). Then specify that you want the bullet points to appear one by one. Click the box under 'delivery' and select 'by bullet' from the drop down menu.

To see what the effect looks like, click 'preview'

Formatting Text Boxes

Click text box to add shown below.

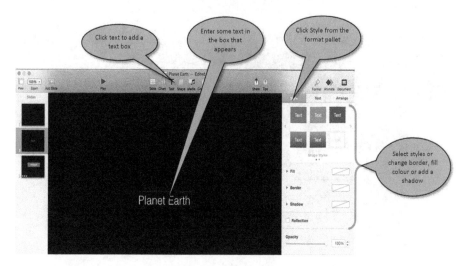

Enter some text into your textbox, and drag it into position on your slide.

You can format your text box by adding borders, changing fonts, changing the background colour, etc To format the border and fill click your text box and on the right hand side of the screen select style.

Formatting Text Inside Textboxes

To change the formatting of the text, for example to change the colour of the text or make it bold.

First select your text in the text box you want to change then click the text icon on the right hand side of your screen as shown below.

From here you can change the font, the font colour, size etc

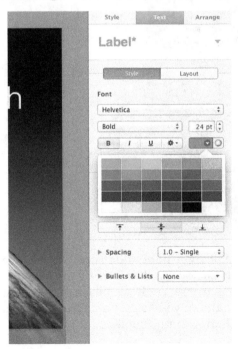

As an example I have changed the colour to dark red and made it bold

Adding Styles to Textboxes

If you wanted to change the background colour (also called fill colour) or add a nice border around the box you can do this by clicking on your text box then selecting style icon located on the top right of your screen

If you look down the right hand side you will see sections: 'Fill' allows you to change the background colour of the text box. 'Border' allows you to add fancy borders such as picture frames and coloured line borders. 'Shadow' allows you to add a drop shadow effect as if the text box is casting a shadow onto the slide.

To change the background colour of the textbox, click fill circled below left and select a colour from the drop down menu.

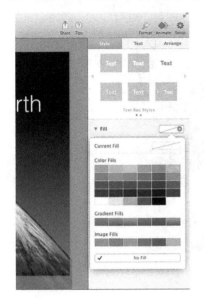 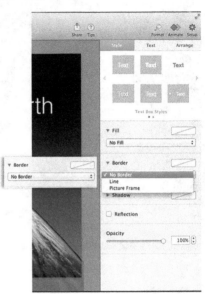

Also if you want to add a border, under the border section click where it says 'no border' as shown above and change it to picture frame

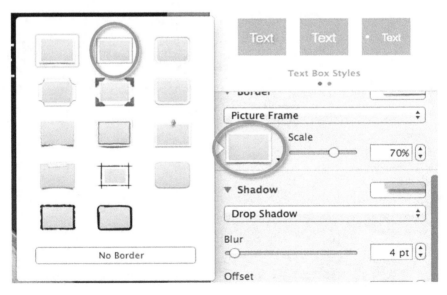

Click the 'choose frame style' button circled above and select a picture frame style from the menu that appears. Change the size by moving the scale slider.

Here is the result of the effect.

Saving

You can save your work onto your documents on your local mac or onto your iCloud Drive as with Pages.

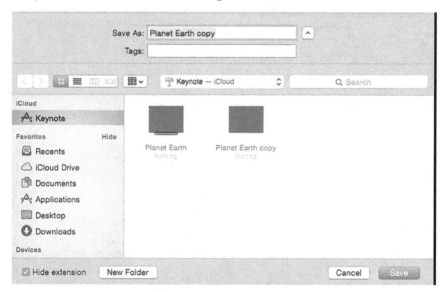

Down the left hand side of the screen you will see some destinations where you can save your file. Take note of Documents under favourites - this is on your mac. Also take note of iCloud at the top, this saves onto your iCloud Drive.

Numbers App

Numbers allows you to create spreadsheets. To numbers keynote, go to launch pad and click the numbers icon.

Once numbers has loaded, you can select a saved file to open.

If you want to create a new spreadsheet, click 'new document' on the bottom left hand side of the window.

From here you can select from a variety of pre-designed templates with different themes, fonts and colours.

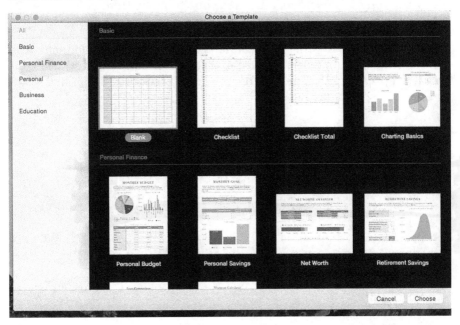

For this example use a blank sheet

Chapter 4: Using Applications

Once you have selected a template you will see the main screen as shown below.

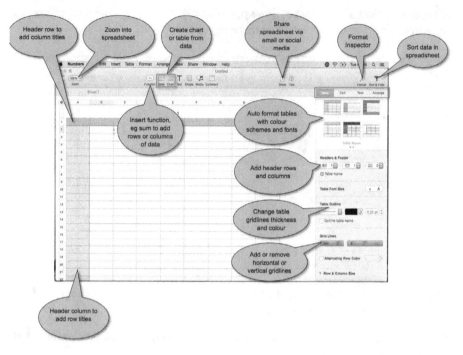

Along the top of the screen you'll see your toolbar. Here you can insert functions, images, tables and charts.

The 'format' icon on the right hand side opens up the sidebar and contains the tools needed to format text, rows, columns and the cells on your spreadsheet. The sidebar is split into tabs: table, cell, text, arrange, as shown below.

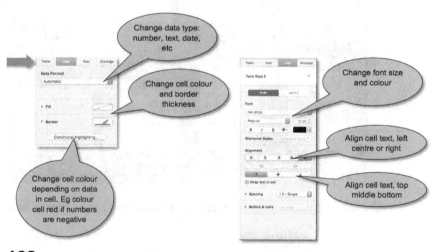

160

Building a Spreadsheet

To begin building your spreadsheet, enter the data into the cells. In this example we are going to build a basic invoice of costs of items

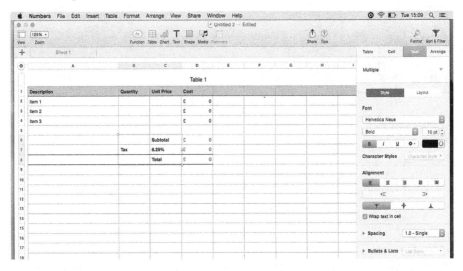

Entering Data

Enter the header cells into the grey row at the top of your spreadsheet. Then enter the rest of the data as shown above.

Change the total cells at the bottom to bold text.

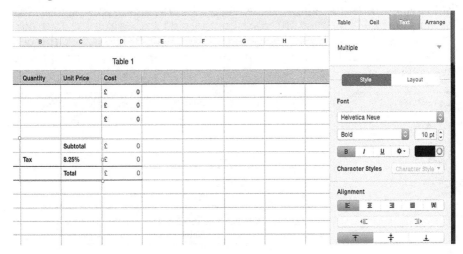

Do this by highlighting them with your mouse and from the cell tab on the right hand side of your screen click Bold.

161

Changing Data Types

Next highlight all the cells that will contain the prices for items, and make them a currency data type. Change it to Pound Sterling or US Dollar.

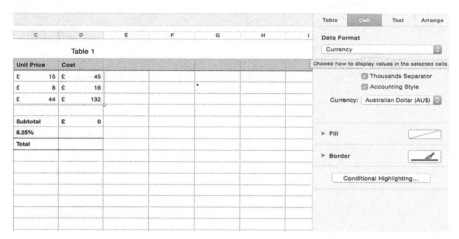

Do this by highlighting your cells as shown above, then from the cell tab on the right hand side, click in the dropdown box under 'data format' and select currency. Further down the tab you can change it to a specific currency depending on which country you are in.

Adding Formulas

Enter a formula to calculate the cost of each item. In the first cell under the heading 'cost' hit your equals sign to begin your formula. Click the cell under quantity, press the asterisk (*) then click the cell under unit price. This means you want to multiply the values in these two cells together.

Description		Quantity	Unit Price	Cost	
Item 1				· ≡ B2 ▾ × C2 ▾ │ ✗ ✓	
Item 2				£ 0	
Item 3				£ 0	
			Subtotal	£ 0	
		Tax	8.25%	£ 0	
			Total	£ 0	

Cost = Quantity * Unit Price.

162

Adding Functions

Now add a function to work out the total cost. For this one use the sum function to add all the values together.

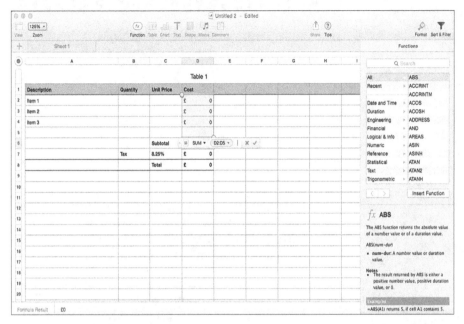

Click in the cell next to subtotal and click the function icon on the tool bar at the top of the screen.

Select 'sum' from the drop down menu. The function will automatically highlight the values to add up.

If it doesn't click where it says D2:D5 this is the cells it will add up. Now select new the cells you want to add.

Saving

You can save your work onto your documents on your local mac or onto your iCloud Drive as with Pages.

Down the left hand side of the screen you will see some destinations where you can save your file. Take note of Documents under favourites - this is on your mac. Also take note of iCloud at the top, this saves onto your iCloud Drive.

The advantage of saving to your iCloud Drive is you can access and edit the documents you have just been working on, on your iPhone or iPad. Or even another mac.

Internet, Email & Communications

Your mac has a wealth of communication apps. MacOS has Safari for browsing the web, an email app to keep track of all your email correspondence. Plus an app for video chat called Facetime.

You can also use iMessage which is similar to the message app on your iPhone/iPad as well as AirDrop for sharing files and mac phone which syncs with your iPhone to allow you to answer calls right from your Mac.

There is also an address book called contacts that stores all your email addresses, phone numbers, Facetime IDs, mailing address and so on. This integrates nicely into your communication apps.

To help you better understand this section, take a look at the video resources. Open your web browser and navigate to the following site:

www.elluminetpress.com/mac-comms/

Lets take a look at the Safari web browser.

Using Safari to Browse the Web

Safari is MacOS Mojave's default web browser. In this iteration of Mac OS, Safari blocks videos from auto playing. This helps bring a friendlier web browsing experience on websites containing adverts. Also in Safari there is a more sophisticated advert tracking prevention to stop websites tracking your browsing habits.

Launching Safari

You will find Safari's icon either on the dock at the bottom of the screen or on your launchpad

This will bring up safari's main screen, which will look similar to the one below.

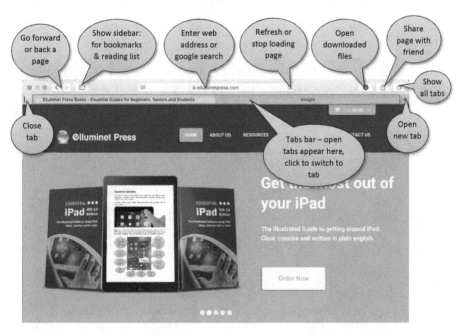

Using Safari

If for example, I wanted to find Elluminet Press's website. Type it into the search bar. You can use a web address or type the keywords.

You can use this technique for anything you want to find. Just start typing it into the address bar. It doesn't have to be a website address, it can be a keyword.

Bookmarking Pages

Bookmarking pages allows you to save websites without having to remember addresses or having to search for them again.

You can just click a button on the bookmarks side bar to revisit the page.

If you have found a website you like or visit often, click the share button.

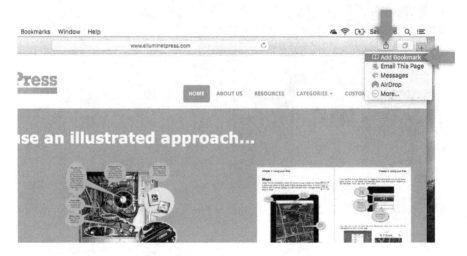

From the menu, select 'add bookmark'.

Choose 'Favourites' from the drop down menu to add bookmark to your bookmark sidebar.

Using the Sidebar

You can access the sidebar by clicking the sidebar icon shown below

From here, you can access favourites/bookmarks and your reading list.

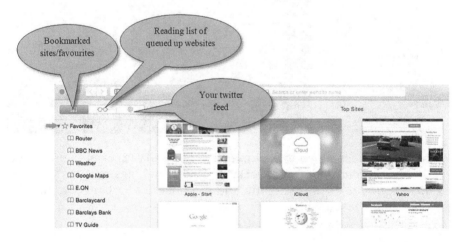

The reading list is where you can queue up a load of websites for reading later, useful when you are not connected to the internet all the time.

Click on the bookmarks icon.

Here you'll see a list of all the sites you have bookmarked. You might need to expand the folders, do this by clicking the small triangle to the left of each folder, indicated with the small red arrow in the above screen.

You can also organise your bookmarks into folders. So for example, all my media websites I could put into a media folder.

To create folders right click on the bookmark sidebar and select 'new folder'.

Give the folder a name. In this case I am naming it 'Media'.

Drag and drop your bookmarks into the folders, as illustrated below.

This helps to keep all your bookmarks organised and easy to find. You could have a folder for your work, interests, hobbies or sites you use to book your holidays/vacations and organise the website bookmarks you use into these folders.

Downloads

Click the downloads icon on the top right of the screen.

Click the small magnifying glass icon next to the download to view it in finder.

Apple Mail

Mail also known as the Mail App or Apple Mail, is an email program included with Mac OS. The main screen will look similar to this...

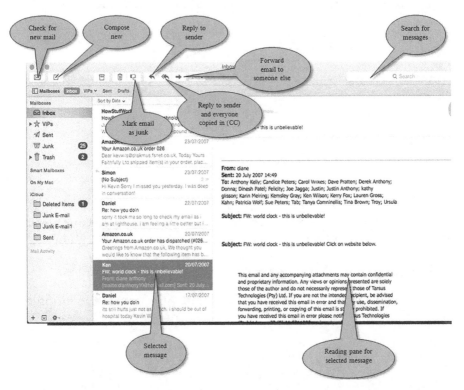

With Apple Mail, you can include all your email accounts into one app. These are listed in the sidebar on the left side of the screen. On the sidebar, you'll also see your different mail boxes: inbox, sent, junk and so on.

In the next pane, you'll see a list of email messages in the mail box you've selected from the sidebar. In the example above, 'inbox' is selected from the sidebar and the email messages are listed in the next pane.

In the far right pane, you'll see a preview of the message you have selected from the centre pane.

To read the message in full within a separate window, double click the message listed in the centre pane.

169

Writing an Email

To send a new email, click the 'compose new email' icon on the top left of your screen. A new blank email window will pop up.

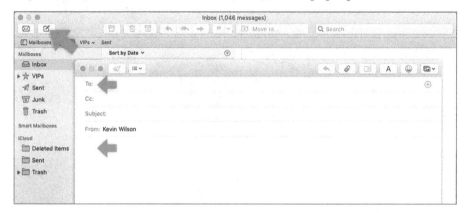

Enter an email address in the 'to' field, add a subject, type your message in the space underneath.

Formatting your Message

Click the font icon that looks like a capital 'A', to reveal the formatting bar.

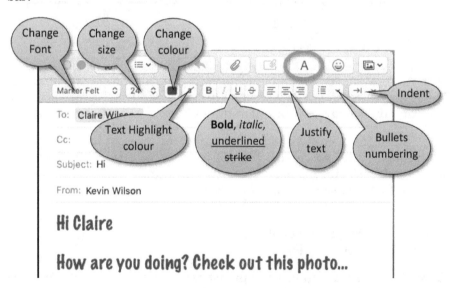

Select the tools from the formatting bar to format your text, change colour, size, alignment, and font. Remember to highlight the text you want to format first, if you've already typed it in.

Add an Emoji

You can add emojis like the ones you see on iMessage, into your email messages. To do this, click the emoji icon on the toolbar.

From the drop down, select the emoji you want to add

Add Attachment

Click the paper clip icon to add an attachment such as a PDF or word document, or a photo you downloaded. Select the file from the dialog box and click 'choose file'.

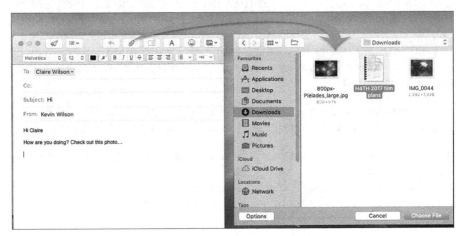

Add Photo from Photos App

If you want to add a photo from your photos app, click the photo icon to pull up your photo albums, as shown above. You can drag and drop any photo into your email to send along.

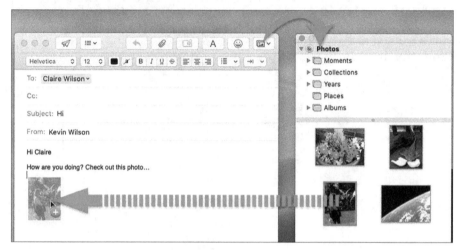

When you're ready to send your message, tap the send icon on the top left.

Mail Drop

MailDrop allows you to send large files by automatically uploading them to your iCloud drive, and then sending a link to the recipient so they can access the file without clogging up the mail server with large files. MailDrop uses your iCloud to store your files, and because iCloud is built into Mail, this means that anyone running Mail on their own Mac will have the file downloaded automatically, just as though it were an ordinary email.

Mail Drop will automatically upload large attachments to iCloud instead of your email provider ie Gmail, Yahoo, or Exchange etc.

If your recipient also uses Mail on a Mac, they'll be able to download the attachment normally, and if not, they'll get a download link that's accessible for 30 days. These attachments don't count towards your iCloud storage limits, which is great. Smaller attachments are sent as normal.

You can open and compose a new email as normal and attach a file. In this example the file is 80MB which is pretty large for an email attachment.

When your recipient receives the email, they'll get a link to click on to access and download the attachment.

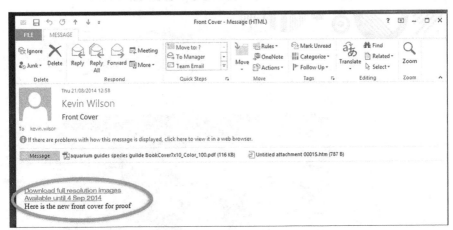

Right click on the attachment link, circled above. From the popup menu select 'download...'.

This should download the attachment into your downloads folder.

Mail Markup

Markup provides a simple way of adding comments and annotations to file attachments in Mail and mostly works with photos or pdf documents.

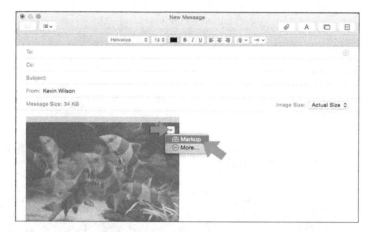

If you send someone a photo for example, in an email you can activate markup mode, by clicking on a small pull-down menu that appears in the top-right corner of the image.

You can then annotate your image, type text, draw lines, circles and hand written notes on the image.

Below is an explanation of what all the different icons do.

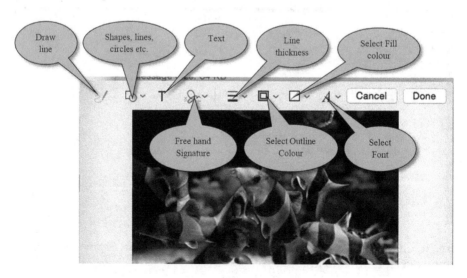

Click the 'draw line' icon.

Now you can draw on your photograph. Try some of the other tools as well. Once you have finished annotating your image click done.

If you don't see the pop-up menu, you may need to enable Markup. To do this go to your system preferences, click extensions,

Click actions, then select the markup checkbox.

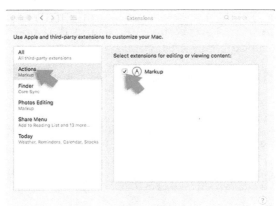

Dealing with Spam & Junk Mail

We all get junk mail - those annoying messages trying to sell you things and just clutter up your inbox with rubbish. Apple Mail has a spam filter where you can filter out these messages.

To enable junk mail filtering, open Apple Mail and go to the 'mail' menu. Select 'preferences'. Click on the 'junk mail' tab.

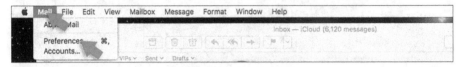

Click the tick box next to 'enable junk mail filtering'.

Now occasionally, the junk mail filter will catch legitimate emails, so it's best to move them to the junk mail folder. To do this, select 'move it to the junk mailbox'. This will keep your inbox clean and move junk to the junk mailbox.

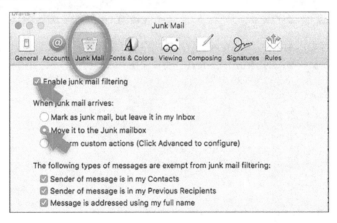

This means that you can check the junk mail box from time to time to check which messages are being filtered and that no important ones have been filtered out.

Contacts

This is your address book and stores all your email, phone numbers, and addresses that you can access from the contacts app itself or through your email, FaceTime, or iMessage.

You'll find the contacts app on your dock, or launchpad. Click the icon to open the app.

You can create contacts, add email addresses and phone numbers. These contacts are synced with all your Apple devices; iPhone, iPad etc.

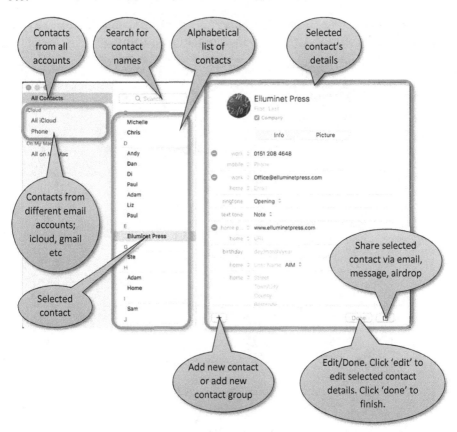

Add a Contact from Scratch

To add a new contact, click the plus sign on the bottom of the contacts window. Select 'new contact' from the drop down menu.

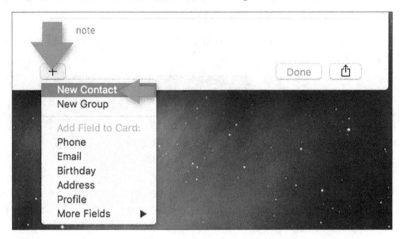

Enter the contact's details - first, last name, phone, email, address and any other information you have in the fields that appear.

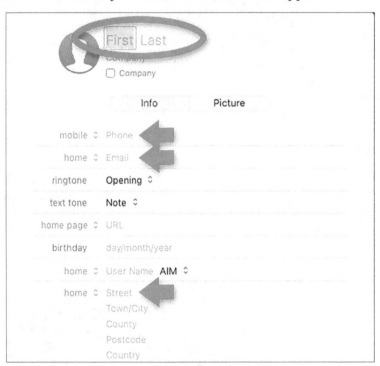

Click 'done' at the bottom when you're finished.

Creating Groups

Groups make it easier to send an email to several different people. This group can be a team. In this example, I'm going to create a group called 'production team' and will contain a list of email address in my team. To create a group, click the plus sign at the bottom, and from the drop down select 'new group'. An untitled group will appear on the left hand side - type in a name.

Now you can drag and drop your contacts into the group.

Now when you start a new email, you'll be able to select the group name rather than having to add all the email addresses manually.

Add Email Contact from Apple Mail

The easiest way to add someone's email address from an email message is to click on the small down-arrow next to their name in the email header, as shown below.

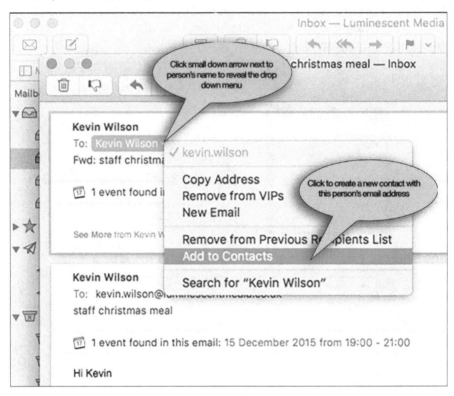

From the popup menu select 'add to contacts'.

This will automatically create an entry in your contacts list with the sender's name and email address from the email you have open.

Take a look at the video demos. Open your web browser and navigate to the following website

www.elluminetpress.com/mac-comms

Facetime

When you open Facetime, you will be prompted to sign in if you haven't already done so.

Once Facetime has opened, you'll see in the main window a preview of your camera. On the left hand side you'll see a darkened panel where you'll find your contacts, history of calls and a search for you to search for people.

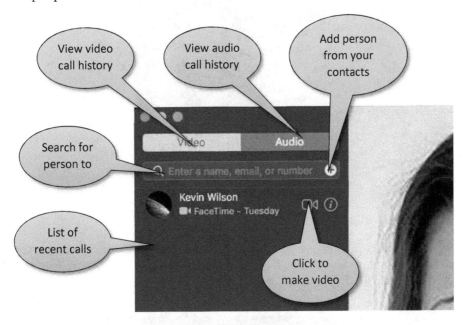

Start typing the person's name you want to Facetime into the search field on the top left of the screen. If the name is in your contacts, then it will appear underneath. Tap the little camera icon next to the name to make a Facetime call.

If you don't see the camera icon next to their name, the chances are they don't have Facetime set up on their side.

In this demonstration, Sophie is logged onto the macbook laptop and she is placing a call to Claire who is logged into the iPad on the left.

Wait for the other person to answer...

When a call comes in on your mac, you'll see a notification on the top right with a preview of your camera. Note, no one will be able to see your camera until you accept the call.

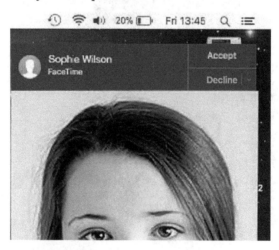

You'll see the name of the person calling on the left hand side of the notification window. Click 'accept' to receive the call, or 'decline' if you're busy or don't want to talk

Once the other person answers, you can have a conversation with them.

Press *CTRL CMD F* for full screen mode on your Mac. Now in the centre of the screen you'll see an image of the person you're calling. On the top left of the screen you'll see a preview of your own camera.

Along the bottom of your screen you'll see three icons. If you don't see them, just move the mouse pointer and they'll re-appear.

The white circle on the left is to take live photos, the red button in the centre ends the call, and the mic icon on the right mutes your microphone.

iMessage

iMessage allows you to send media rich text messages to other iPhones, Macs and some other smart phones. You can find iMessage on your Dock at the bottom of the screen

You can send a new message by clicking on the new message icon, then in the new message window click the + sign to add your recipients.

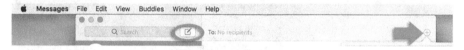

From the drop down, select the contact from the list.

The message window will open up. Type your message in field at the bottom of the screen. You'll see a message transcript in the main window.

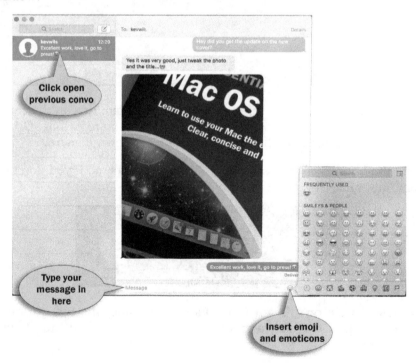

Click on the smiley face on the right hand side of the message field to add your emojis.

In the demo below, you can see one user is logged onto an iPhone and the other user is logged onto a Mac.

You can send files in your messages. To do this, click and drag a file, photo, or video from the desktop or finder directly into the message window.

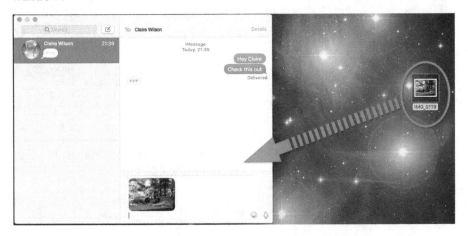

Air Drop

AirDrop is a service that enables users to transfer files to another supported devices ie Mac computer and iPad or iPhone without using email or a USB stick or external hard drive.

You can share pages from Safari. To do this, click the share icon and select 'AirDrop'.

This will share the current web page with other AirDrop users close by.

You can also share documents or photos in finder. To do this, right click on the file, click 'share', then select 'AirDrop'.

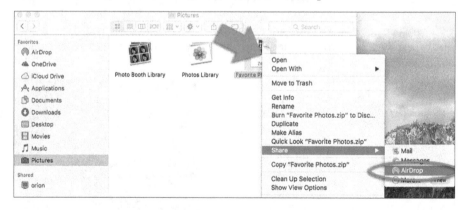

Your friend will see something like this in the Air Drop folder in Finder. Click 'save and open' on the prompt dialog box to view.

Mac Phone

You can answer calls on your Mac if you have an iPhone. For this feature to work, you'll need to be connected to the same WiFi network, and signed in with the same iCloud account on both your Mac and iPhone. Then you'll need to enable the feature. On your iPhone, open the settings app and select 'phone'.

Turn on 'Calls on Other Devices'. You'll see the other Apple devices you'll receive your iPhone calls on.

Now, on your Mac, open the FaceTime app. Go to the preferences menu on the top left. Make sure 'Calls from iPhone' is selected.

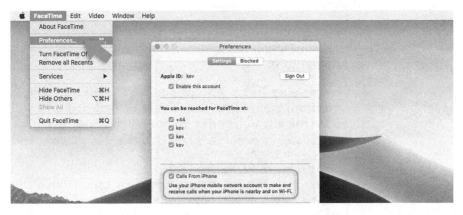

Whenever you are on your Mac and your iPhone rings, you can pick up the call. You'll see a notification appear on the top right of the screen.

Click 'accept' to answer the call.

Chapter 6

Using Multimedia

Photos has more features that are similar to the Photos app on the iPad and iPhone borrowing some of the same style of operation.

You can import photos from your iPhone and sync them with your Photos library as well as import them from a digital camera.

You can create some very nice looking photo books, greetings cards and slide shows all with your own photographs.

Photos also has features such as intelligent scene detection, face, place and object recognition and will automatically categorise your photos allowing you to search using people's names, names of places, and objects.

There is also a 'memories' feature, that will automatically group your photos into slideshows for you to enjoy and share with your friends.

To help you better understand this section, take a look at the video resources. Open your web browser and navigate to the following site:

www.elluminetpress.com/mac-mm/

Photos App

The Photo App is a great way to store and manipulate your photographs taken from a digital camera. First, enable the sidebar, if it isn't already enabled; makes navigating easier.

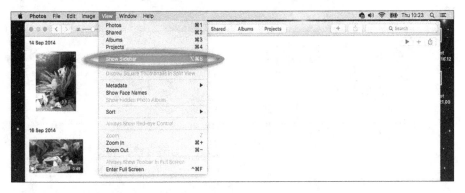

You can create albums and slide shows, you can email a photo to a friend, post them onto Facebook, you can even put together your own album send it to apple and they will print you out a copy and post it to you, these are great for family albums or wedding albums and other special occasions.

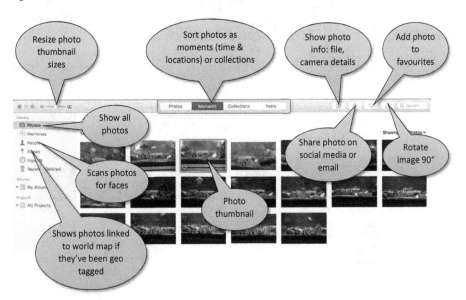

Photo app allows you to organise and manage all your photographs, create calendars, upload photos to websites, create greetings cards, slide shows to music etc.

Importing your Photos

Most digital cameras connect to your computer using a USB cable, as shown below.

Open photos from launch pad and connect your camera. Photos will detect the camera connected and open up the import screen.

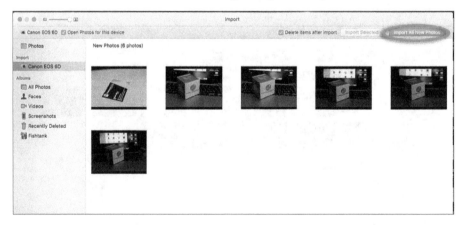

I found it best to delete them off the camera once imported into the Photo library. This means I have a clean camera for the next time I want to take photographs.

To do this, click the tick box next to 'delete items after import'.

This helps eliminate duplicate photographs in the library.

Now go to 'photos' in your library on the left hand side of the screen

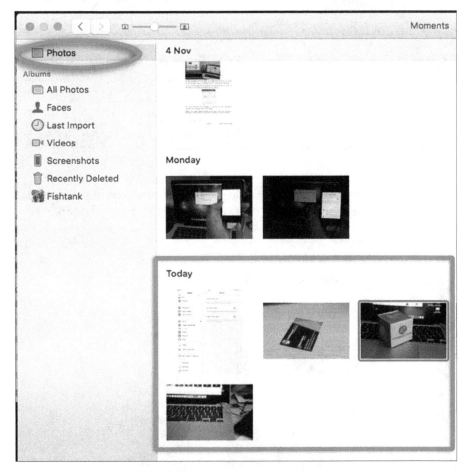

You should now be able to see all the photos you have just imported.

Now this is where you can put them into albums, create slide shows, upload to Facebook, email them to friends or create prints.

Creating Folders and Albums

The photos app allows you to organize your photos into albums (shown in green). You can in turn organise all your albums into folders (shown in blue).

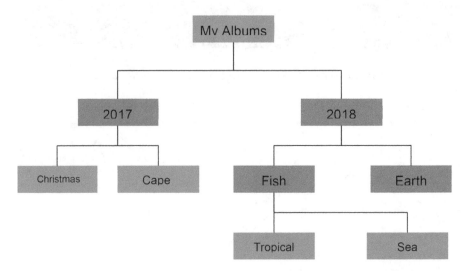

To create a blank folder or album, hover your mouse pointer over 'my albums'. Click the plus sign that appears. From the popup menu select 'album' to create a new album, or 'folder' to create a new folder.

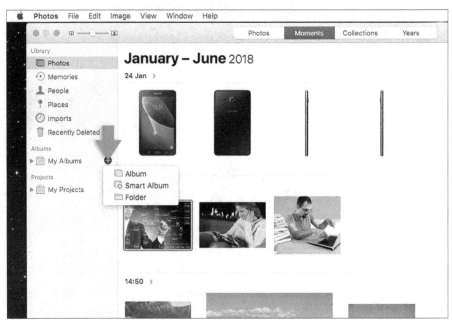

I'm going to create a folder called '2017' to store my albums from that year.

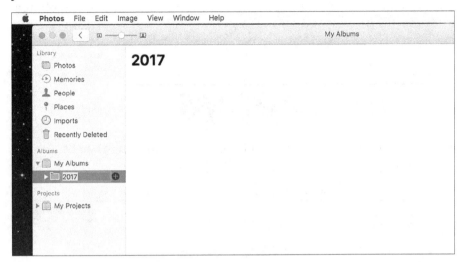

Now, you can't create albums within albums, but you can organize your albums into folders.

Inside the 2017 folder, I'm going to create an album called 'cape'.

If you want to create another folder inside 2017, select '2017', then click the plus sign and select 'folder'.

Note that you can't create albums inside of other albums. You can create folders inside folders, then you can create albums inside these folders.

Adding Photos to Albums

To add photos to your albums. Open your photos library - click 'photos' from the 'library' section on the top left.

Select the photos you want to add. Then click and drag the photos into the albums on the left hand panel under 'my albums'.

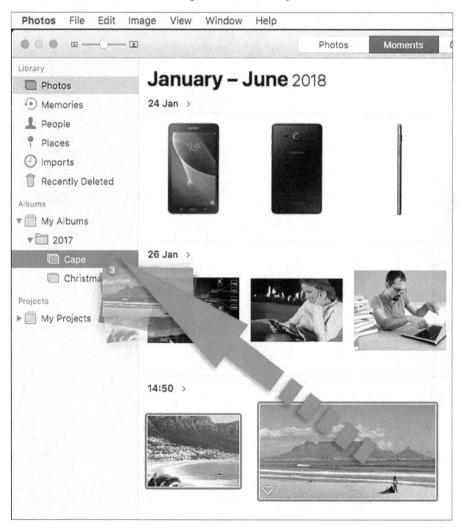

Manipulating & Enhancing Photos

A common problem I have come across, when taking photographs with a pocket digital camera, is sometimes photos can come out a bit dark.

To edit the photo, double click on it. Click 'edit' on the top right of the screen.

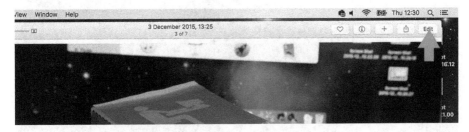

Down the right hand side of the screen, you'll see a list of operations you can perform on your photograph.

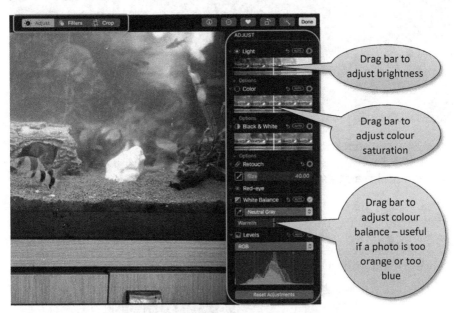

For example, to change the brightness of the image, select 'adjust' from three options on the top, centre of the screen.

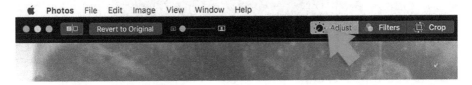

Under the adjustments on the right hand side, you'll see one called 'light'. Underneath you'll see a gradient going from a dark image to a light image and a slider somewhere in the middle. Click and drag this slider toward the light, to lighten the image.

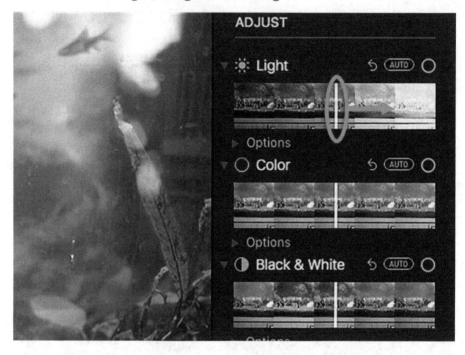

You can do the same for the 'color'; saturate and desaturate the colours. You can also click 'auto' on these adjustments and photos app will make a guess.

If you scroll further down the adjustment controls, you'll see some more advanced features.

You can change the white balance, this is good for adjusting photos that have a distinctive orange or blue tone to them.

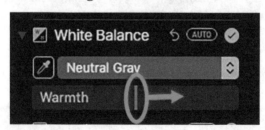

Neutral gray is usually one to use, however if you are adjusting a portrait of someone, click this box and change it to 'skin tone'.

If you scroll further down the adjustment options, you'll see some more advanced features.

Drag points to adjust black, shadows, mid tones, highlights and white

Select a primary colour and adjust hue, saturation, and brightness for each

Remove image noise, useful for dark photos you've tried to brighten up

Click and drag the sliders underneath the names of the effects to adjust the photograph.

Adding Filters

Filters give your photograph a predefined look, such as changing your photo to a sepia or black and white look; make the colours more vivid, warm or dramatic.

Double click on your image and select 'edit' from the top right. Select 'filters' from the options on the top centre of the screen.

Down the right hand side you'll see some filters. Click on the icons to apply the filter.

Click 'done' to save.

Sharing Photos

You can share your photos from your Mac and post them to any social media platform you have signed up to.

From the main screen, select the images you want to post to your social media account.

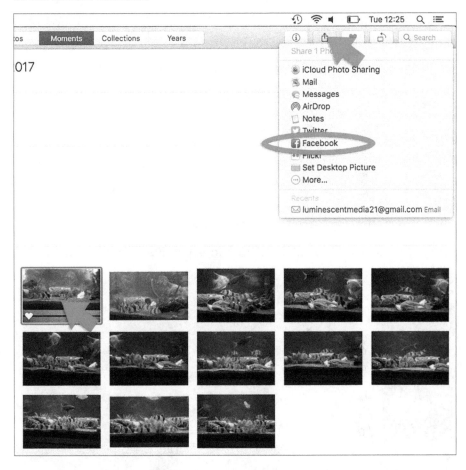

To select multiple images, as shown above, hold down the cmd key while you click the image.

Click the sharing icon on the top right of your screen, shown by the arrow in the screen above. Select your social media, in this example, Facebook.

If you haven't added your Facebook account, click 'add account' when prompted.

If you haven't set up your accounts, Photos app will prompt you for your login username and password. Enter these when prompted.

Click 'next', then click 'sign in'. Close the window and return to Photos.

From Photos, select the share icon and select Facebook.

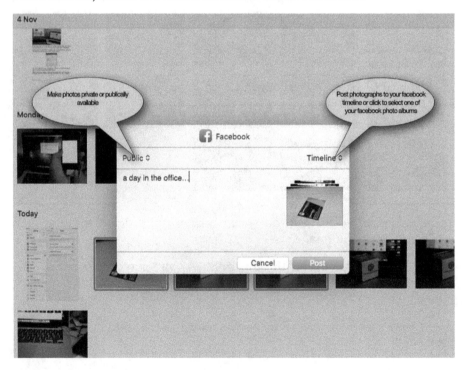

Creating Photobooks

Select your photos from the main screen, hold down the CMD key to select multiple photographs.

To create a book, right click on the selection. From the drop down menu, go down to 'create' and select 'book'.

Choose the format you would like your album printed in. Click 'select' under the one you want.

There are a number of templates to choose from. Double click the one you want.

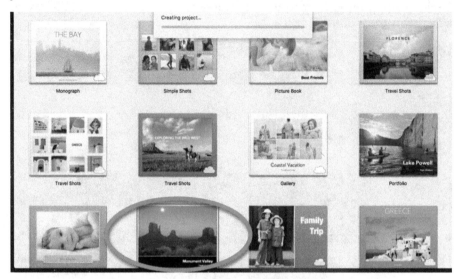

In the next screen, you'll notice photos has put all your images into the pages. You can leave the photos in this order or if you prefer, click 'clear placed photos' and all the photos will be removed and placed on the dock at the bottom of the window.

From here you can click and drag the photos onto the pages in the order and position you want them.

Double click on the thumbnails to enlarge them to edit text and adjust layouts.

You can adjust the layout if you want more photos on one page or a photo and a text field if you want to add some explanation/story to your book.

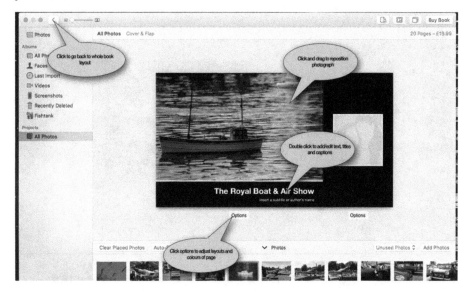

You can do this by clicking 'options' and selecting a template from the layout options.

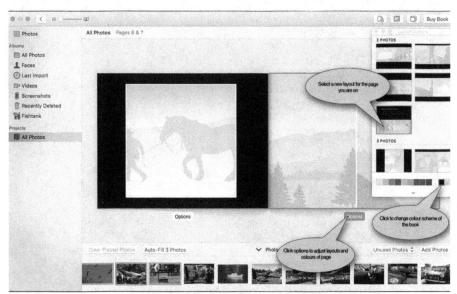

Once you are happy with the book, click 'buy book' to order your book as a hard copy printed album.

Chapter 6: Using Multimedia

Click 'Add shipping address' type in or select your address and click 'place order'

These make nice gifts at weddings, birthdays and special events.

Creating Slide Shows

Select the photos you want, hold down the CMD key to select multiple photographs. Right click on the selection.

From the drop down menu select 'slideshow', go down to 'create' and select 'slideshow'.

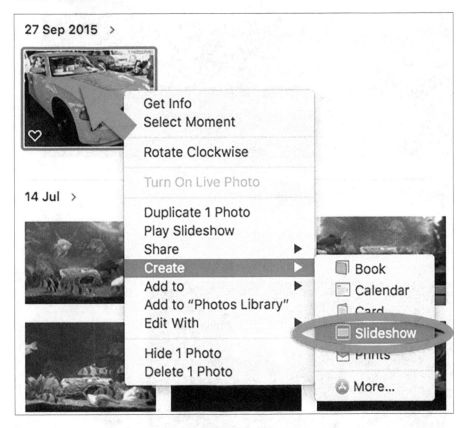

Give your slideshow a name

Double click the title text to edit the title.

Add some effects by clicking on the effects button on the right hand side, circled below far right.

In this example, I am going to apply a nice vintage photo look.

Click the music icon on the right hand side, indicated by the arrow, to add some music. You can add music from photos or you can use music from your iTunes library.

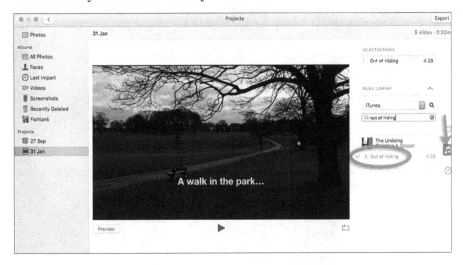

Hit the play button to run your slideshow. Now you won't have to bore your friends and family with your holiday/vacation pictures - you can create a more interesting slideshow.

Ordering Prints

Select the photographs you want to print, hold down the CMD key to select multiple photographs. It's best to order at least 10 to make the order worthwhile for the cost of printing and shipping.

Right click on your selection, go down to 'create' and from the slideout select 'prints'.

Ordering prints is like using a kiosk at a photo store where you can order professionally printed photographs. This feature of Photos works in a similar way.

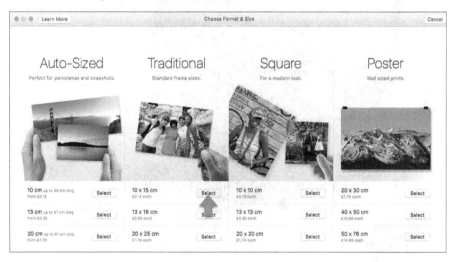

From the list, select the size of the photographs you want to print. Select a glossy finish on the top right hand side of the screen.

All the photos you have selected will be scaled and cropped to the size of the photographs you have selected on the previous screen.

You can change sizes by right clicking on the image and selecting a different size from the 'change size' sub menu.

Once you are done, click 'order prints', enter your payment and address details. Then click 'place order'.

They'll post the prints to your address. You can frame and display them in your home if you wish.

Printing Photos

To print photos, select the photos you want to print.

From the 'file' menu, then select 'print'.

From the print preview screen, select 'custom' from the layout options on the right hand side

Under photo size, change the size of the photos to 9cm by 14cm. This will crop and fit four 9x14 photos onto a page.

Click 'print' when you're done.

Greeting Cards

Select your photograph to make your card. In this example, I am going to use a nice coffee image.

Right click on your photo, go down to 'create' and from the slideout select 'card'.

Click 'select' under the size and style of card you want.

Select a category of templates using the drop down box on the top centre of your screen. Double click on a template, in this case I'm going to choose 'holiday colors'.

You can also select between landscape cards and portrait cards.

Click on the text on the front page and click 'options'. Here you can change the font, colour from the 'text options' box. You can type in your own message.

Click on the photograph and choose a filter, also crop your photograph so it fits the card.

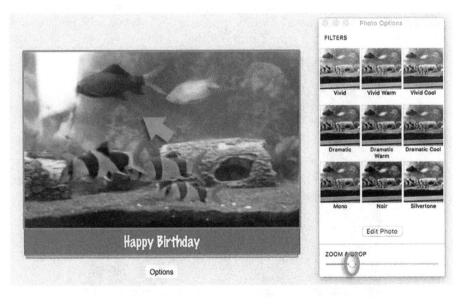

Drag the slider left and right, until the image is nicely positioned on the card.

Click on 'inside' then click on the text box circled at the bottom and enter your message. You can also change fonts and colours using the 'text options' box on the right hand side of the window.

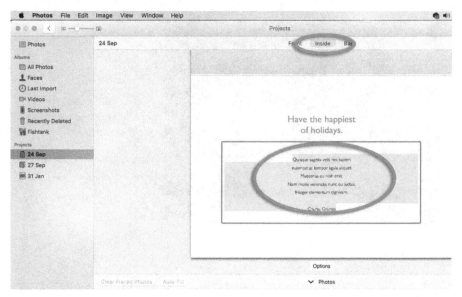

Once you are happy, click 'buy card' on the top right of the screen. Add your recipient's address and click 'place order'. Apple will mail you a hard copy card you or a friend can display at home.

A Gift Calendar

You can make a calendar using your own photographs. Pick 12 photos of you and your family or of a special occasion and present it to someone as a special gift.

Select your photos from the main screen. Hold down the CMD key to select multiple photographs.

Right click on your selection, go down to 'create' and select 'calendar'.

Select a 12 month calendar - one photo on each page. Select 'calendar'

Then select the start month and year. Usually starts from January.

Hit continue

Select a style you like from the templates.

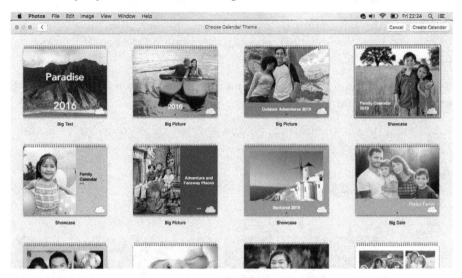

You'll see Photos has inserted all your photographs.

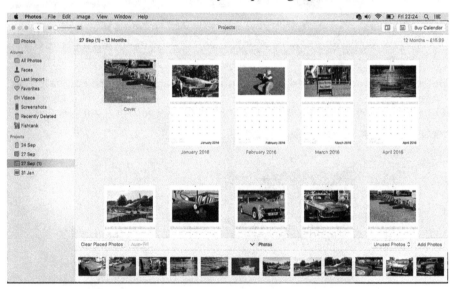

You can click on the thumbnails to change the layout. Click and drag photos from different pages to other pages to re-arrange them.

Click and drag photos from the strip of photos along the bottom onto the pages to replace photos.

Once you are happy click 'buy calendar'.

Faces

The faces feature scans your photographs for recognisable faces and will show them as thumbnails on the people section. You can find the people section by selecting 'people' from the list on the left hand side of the screen.

In this section, you can add names to the thumbnails to help the Photos App identify people, as illustrated below.

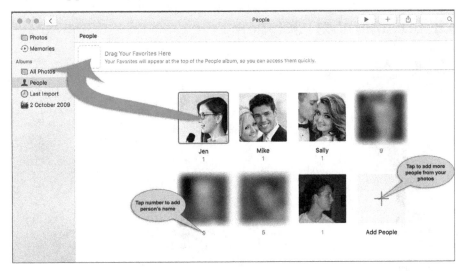

You can drag the people you know best, such as friends and family, to the favourites section at the top of the page so you can find them quickly.

Once you have added all the names, you can start searching for people by name using the smart search feature.

Places

Photos App will tag your photos and record where your photo was taken, this is called geo tagging. If you have location services set on your iPhone, it will tag the photographs

You can also assign locations if your camera hasn't got a geo tagging feature. Select your images, right click on the selection and click 'get into'.

Click on 'assign a location' and type in the name of the city or location the photo was taken. Select the closest match from the drop down menu of suggested locations.

Now when you select 'locations' from the sidebar on the main screen, you'll see your photos appear across the world map according to the locations they were taken in.

Memories

Memories are short slide show movies Photos App automatically creates, based on the time and place they were taken. You can add music and transitions between the photos to spice up your memories.

Create your Own Memory

To create your own memories, go to the 'Photos' tab and select all the photos you want to appear in your memory. You can select multiple photos by holding down the cmd key on your keyboard while selecting your photos.

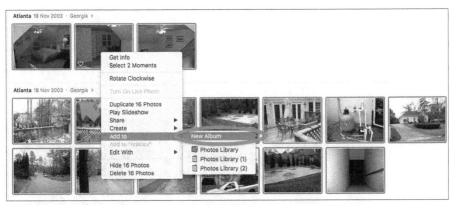

Right click on your selection, click 'add to' and select 'new album' from the slideout. Give the album a name, I'm going to call mine 'Thanks'. Your albums will show up under the albums section on the left hand side of the screen.

At the top of your album, click 'Show as Memory'. Scroll right to the bottom of the page and click 'add to memories'.

Now when you go back to your memories section, you'll see your album has been added to your memories.

Click the play button on the top right of your screen and select a theme and some music; you can use the built in songs or tracks from your iTunes library.

If you want a song from your iTunes library, click the music tab and select a track.

Once you have done that, click 'play slideshow'.

Share a Memory

You can also share your slideshow memories with friends and family on email or social media.

To do this click the share icon on the top right of your screen.

From the drop-down menu select, mail to email it, facebook to post it to your facebook account, messages to send over iMessage and so on.

In this example, I am going to post it on facebook.

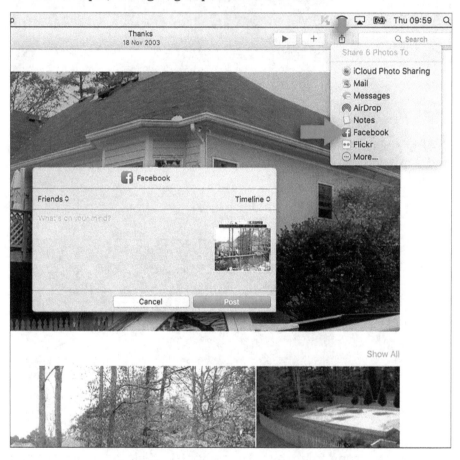

In the pop up box that appears, add a message to your post and click 'post' when you're done.

You can use the same procedure to send via email, and iMessage and so on.

Smart Search

Apple have added some interesting algorithms to their Photo App recently; ones that can recognise faces, objects and locations, all from within the smart search feature.

The smart search feature scans and analyses your photos to determine what objects the images contain; so it will try identify places, objects, animals, faces and will tag them accordingly.

This makes finding and grouping your photos so much easier. For example if I wanted to find all the photos in my library of cats, I can just type 'cats' into the search field.

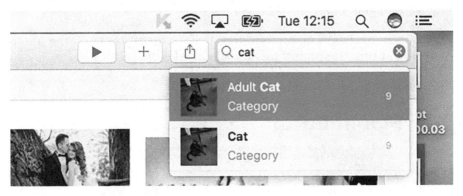

From the categories that show up in the results, I can select one and Photos App will show me all the photographs I have of cats.

Continuity Camera

To use Continuity Camera, you will need to sign into all your Apple devices with the same Apple ID (eg Mac and iPhone). Also they will need to be connected to the same Wi-Fi network with Bluetooth enabled.

You can use continuity camera to quickly snap a photo with your iPhone or iPad and have it appear instantly on your Mac. This can be useful if you're writing a Pages document and need to insert a quick photo of something. You can also use continuity camera as a scanner, to scan in photos, documents etc.

In this demo, I'm going to insert a photo taken with an iPhone directly into a Pages document.

First open your Pages document. Right click where you want the photo to appear. From the popup menu, select 'take photo'.

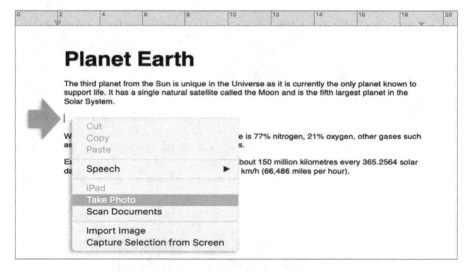

You'll see a place-holder appear asking you to take the photo with your device

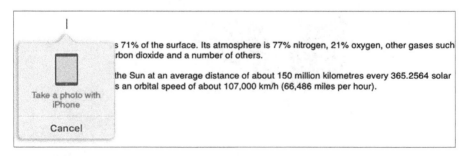

The camera app will open on your iPhone. Line up your shot, then tap the white circle to take the photo.

The photo will appear in the document.

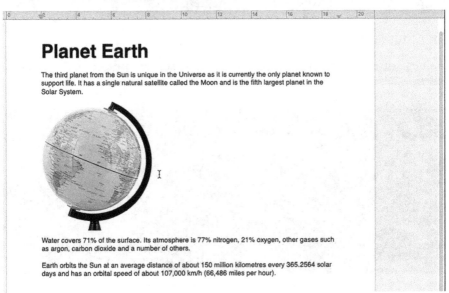

You can also scan documents using this feature, just choose 'scan documents' from the drop down menu instead of 'take photo'.

iMovie

iMovie is great for editing together your home movies. Perhaps you've just come back from your vacation/holiday, maybe a family member or friend has just got married, or maybe just collecting precious memories of your kids. You will find iMovie on your dock or in finder - if not, go to the app store and download it.

Importing Footage from your Camera

Connect the camera to your Mac with the USB cable. Turn your camera on and set it to 'PC Connect Mode' if required.

Now on your Mac, launch iMovie. Go to the file menu and select 'new movie'.

Tap 'import media'.

Select your camera on the top left of the screen under the 'cameras' section. You'll see a thumbnail list of all the clips on your camera.

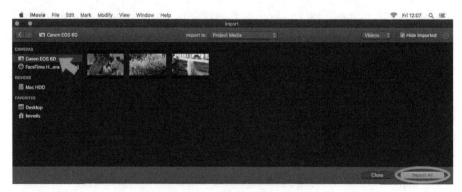

Select which video clips to import then click 'import selected'.

To import all clips click 'import all'.

Importing Footage from your iPhone

To import video clips from your iPhone or iPad, you'll need to connect your device to your Mac using the USB cable.

Plug the cable into the bottom of your device, then plug the other end into a spare USB port on your Mac. You'll need to unlock your device with your Touch ID/Face ID, or passcode. When you do, you'll see a 'trust' prompt appear. Tap 'trust' to allow your Mac to access the media on your device.

Now on your Mac, launch iMovie. Go to the file menu and select 'new movie'.

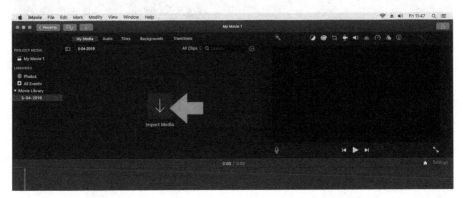

Tap 'import media'.

Chapter 6: Using Multimedia

Select your device on the top left of the screen under the 'cameras' section. In this example, my iPhone is called 'ElluminetPress', so I'd select that one.

Here you can preview any clips and select the ones you want. Click 'import all' to import all your clips to your Mac.

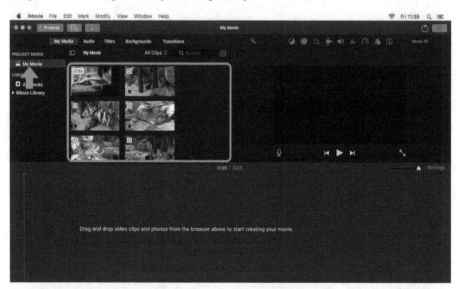

Once imported, you'll see all your clips in the project window.

Now you can start to drag and drop your clips into the timeline at the bottom of the screen to create your movie.

Adding Clips

To begin editing, click and drag a clip from your photo library or imported footage to the time line at the bottom of the screen.

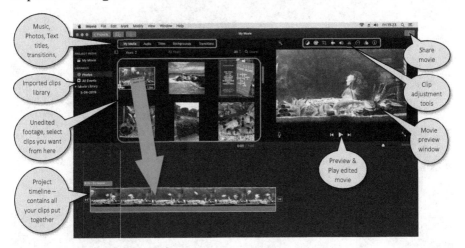

Continue to add the clips you want to appear in your movie. You can also trim or cut out bits of the clips you don't want. For example, I want to add a part of the clip below. If you hover your mouse pointer over the clip, you'll see a yellow box appear with two handles either side - this is your trim box.

Click and drag the handle to mark the part of the clip you want. You'll see a preview of the clip play as you move your mouse - this is so you can see where in the clip you currently are.

Do the same for the end of the clip also.

Click and drag the clip you just trimmed to the time line. The clip will snap into place at the end.

Do the same with any other clips you want to add to your video.

Adding Titles

To add a title, select 'titles' from the icons along the top of the screen.

Click and drag the title you want to the position on the timeline where the title is to appear.

On the preview window on the right hand side, you'll see the title text markers. Type in your titles here.

Use the tool controls along the top to change font, size, colour, and so on.

Adding Music

To add a title, select 'audio' from the icons along the top of the screen.

From your iTunes music library, click and drag the track you want to the position on the timeline where the music is to start.

Transitions

You can also add transition effects between the clips. You can add a crossfade, wipe, or cut, along with various other transitions.

To add a transition, click the 'transition' icon along the top of the screen.

Drag the transition you want to one of the gaps between the clips on your timeline

To change the length of the transition, right click on the transition marker, and select 'precision editor' from the menu.

Now click on the yellow marker and drag it to the right to increase the length of the transition.

Click 'close precision editor', when you're done.

Animations

The only decent animation that is available is the map or globe. This is a nice feature to include in vacation/holiday videos, as you can set the location on the map to indicate where you've travelled to. You can also add backgrounds to titles.

To add an animation, click the 'backgrounds' icon along the top of the screen. Click and drag one of the map/globe animations to the position on the video the animation is to appear.

Double click on the animation in the timeline. You'll see a preview of the animation in the preview screen on the right hand side. Here you can customise it

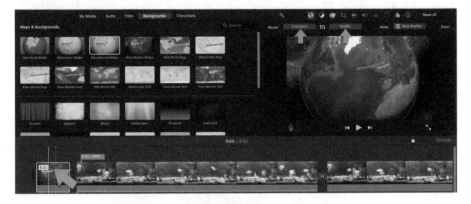

Add your travel destinations in the route options at the top of the preview window.

Now when you play the animation, you'll see a map of your route.

iTunes

iTunes allows you to organize and manage all your music. You can purchase individual tracks or albums from the music store or you can import music from an ordinary music CD.

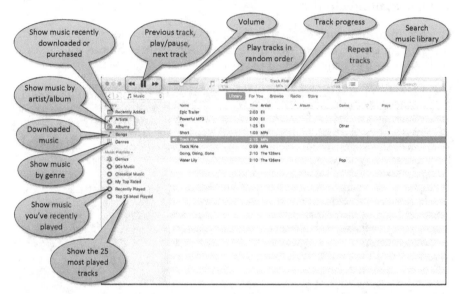

When using iTunes, I find it easier to use with the sidebar showing as above. Click the 'view' menu and select 'show sidebar'.

You can see all the music in iTunes by clicking on 'library'. If you have an Apple Music subscription, click 'for you' to see Apple Music's recommendations according to your music tastes. Similarly click 'browse' to have a look through Apple Music's library, with your subscription, you can listen to any track you want.

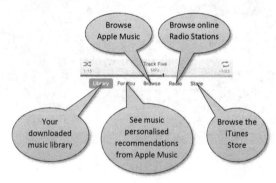

If you don't have an Apple Music subscription, you can still buy tracks. You can buy them from the iTunes Store. To do this click 'store'.

Plugging in an iPhone or iPad

Connect your iPad to a USB port on your computer using the iPad lighting cable.

When you plug in your device, another icon will appear allowing you to view content and change sync settings for your device.

Here you can check for updates. Click 'check for updates' to do this. Press the option key and click 'check for updates' if you have downloaded a restore image (IPSW).

You can restore your device to its factory settings if you have problems with it. To do this click 'restore iPhone/iPad'. This will wipe your data, apps, music and settings, so you'll need to restore from a backup if you do this.

You can also view music, add/remove apps or photos by clicking on the links down the left hand side of the screen. This will show you what is currently installed on your device.

Add Music to iPhone or iPad

To add music, plug your device into a USB port on your computer using the lightning cable.

Find a track in your library, right click on that track and in the menu that appears, go down to 'Add to Playlist'.

You can select multiple tracks by holding down the CMD key while clicking the tracks. Then right click on one of the selected tracks.

Then in the slide out menu select the name of your iPhone.

Burn a Playlist to a CD

When adding music to your playlist, as a guide, keep an eye on the status bar at the bottom middle of the main window, an 80 minute CD will hold 1.2 hours. If you go over this, you'll need more than one CD.

Once you have compiled your playlist, right click on it in the pane on the left hand side. Click burn playlist to disc.

'Use Sound Check' is useful when you have made a compilation of songs from different albums. It makes sure all the songs are at the same volume level, so you don't have to raise or lower the volume too much when you're listening to the CD in the car or on a CD player.

Make sure 'Gap Between Songs' is set to none or automatic.

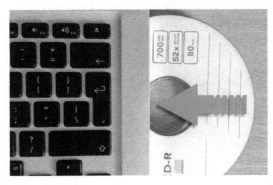

Insert a blank CD-R then click burn.

Import from a CD

CDs are a bit old school now days but many of us still have large collections of CDs with music we all enjoy listening to.

You can import music from a CD by inserting the disc into your drive.

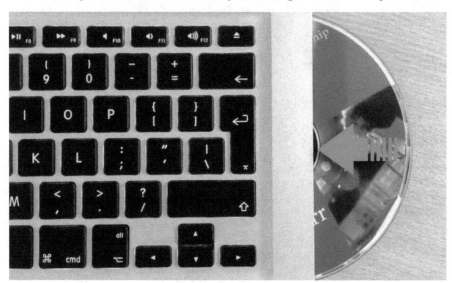

iTunes will scan the CD and ask you if you want to import the tracks.

99% of the time iTunes will be able to find the track names and album art for you.

Click 'yes' to import the tracks into your iTunes library.

iTunes will add your tracks to your music library. You can find them by going to 'music' section of your library.

iTunes Store

You can buy music albums and individual tracks, as well as films, tv programmes, books and podcasts.

Click 'Store' to open the iTunes Store.

Searching the Store

Once you are signed in type the songs you want in Search Store field on the right hand side of the screen.

Click on the price to download the song. Once the songs are downloaded you will find then in your recently added playlist.

Films & TV Programmes

You can download your favourite films and TV programmes directly to your Mac from the iTunes Store.

Open the iTunes store. Over on the right hand side of your screen, you'll see some links. Click the small arrow next to 'music' as shown below.

From the popup menu select 'films'. This will change to the films section of the iTunes store. Here you'll see all the latest films that are out to rent or buy. Tap on one of the films to see more details and watch a trailer.

You can also search for your favourite films using the search field on the top right of the screen. Click on a thumbnail in the results to view details on the movie

Here you can read some details about the movie: plot, trailers, reviews and ratings.

On the left hand side you can buy the movie or rent it. If you buy the movie you can keep it as long as you like in your films library.

Once you've rented your movie, you have 30 days to start watching and once you've started you must finish watching your movie within 48 hours.

You can also watch trailers and features promoting the movie.

Apple Music

Apple Music is a music streaming service and for a monthly subscription fee, you can listen to any music that is available in the iTunes Store.

£9.99 a month gets you full access to the iTunes store and many radio stations available. This is an individual account and allows only one account access to the iTunes Store.

£14.99 a month gets you full access to the iTunes store and radio stations and allows up to 6 people to sign in and listen to their music. This is ideal for families.

To get started, make sure you have updated to the latest iTunes on your Mac.

In the top-left corner, click the Music icon.

Click 'For You'.

Then click 'Start 3-Month Free Trial' or 'Join Apple Music' or 'get 3 months free'; whatever Apple have decided to call it.

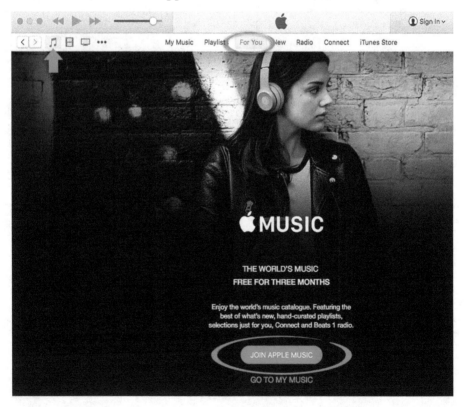

Choose a membership programme and sign in with your Apple ID

Select the genres you like. Click next. Select the artists you like. Click Done.

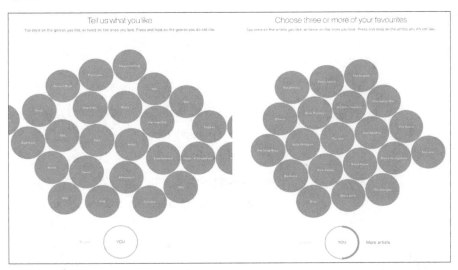

Select whether you want to upload your iTunes library. This is the library of music you have downloaded from iTunes and is stored on your Mac. Uploading this will allow you to access this library on all your devices (iPad, iPhone and so on).

Search

Now, you can search for any artist, band or song you can think of. To do this, on iTunes's home screen, type an artist's/album name into the search field on the top right.

Click on the name in the search list. You will see a whole selection of albums, singles and songs you can listen to. Click on an album or song.

From here you can click on a song to listen to it, or you can build your own playlists.

Browse

You can browse through the latest releases from your favourite artists and bands.

This section is split into new music, curated playlists, top charts and genres.

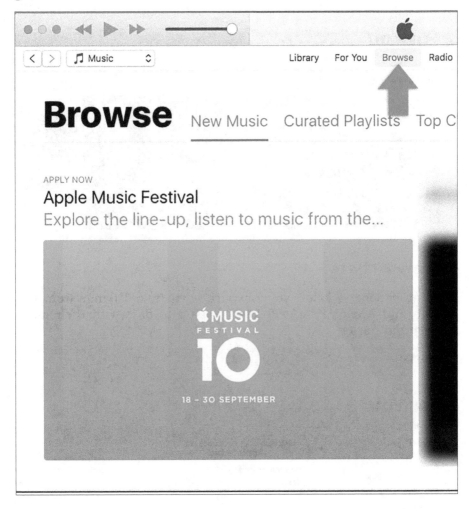

Click on the tracks and thumbnails to view and album listen to a song.

Recommendations for You

Apple Music keeps track of your activity, the music you listen to and makes recommendations according to what it thinks you will be interested in.

Follow Artists

You can choose to follow your favourite artists and bands from this section and Apple Music will keep you up to date with their latest activity and releases.

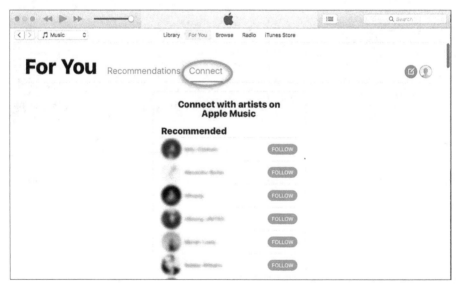

Creating Playlists

To create a new playlist, click the + sign in the bottom left hand side of the screen. This will add a playlist to the library. Type in the name you want to call it.

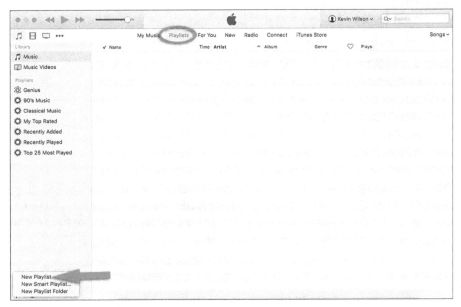

Adding Songs

Right click your mouse on the song you want to add.

From the drop down menu that appears, select 'add to playlist'

Then select your playlist you want to add your song to. If you have no playlists, tap 'new playlist' and give it a name.

Tap done.

Maintaining your Mac

Macs are said to have better security, however they are still susceptible to malware, phishing and viruses, so its wise to take precautions when browsing the web or opening emails.

It's a myth that Macs don't get viruses, so make sure you're protected, especially when you are shopping or banking online.

In this section we'll take a look at some of the security aspects of Macs and how to go about putting it into practice.

We'll also look at ways to update your mac and keep it running smoothly.

To help you better understand this section, take a look at the video resources. Open your web browser and navigate to the following site:

www.elluminetpress.com/mac-sys/

Firewalls

A firewall helps prevent unauthorised access to your Mac by monitoring incoming and outgoing network traffic and connections according to a set of rules. A firewall won't protect you against malware and viruses, so adequate anti-virus software is still necessary but it *is* your first line of defence against a hacker trying to gain access to your computer, or some malicious software trying to send data.

To set up your firewall, open the system preferences app and click 'Security & Privacy',

Click on the firewall tab.

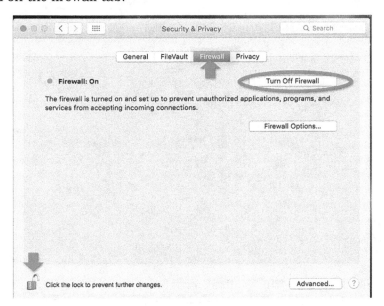

Click on the padlock and enter your admin password to unlock the settings, then click 'Turn On Firewall'.

Gatekeeper

Gatekeeper is a feature introduced in Mountain Lion and OS X Lion that checks for malware to help protect your Mac from misbehaving apps downloaded from the Internet.

Click the Apple menu on the top left of your screen, then select System Preferences. From the System Preferences window select Security & Privacy.

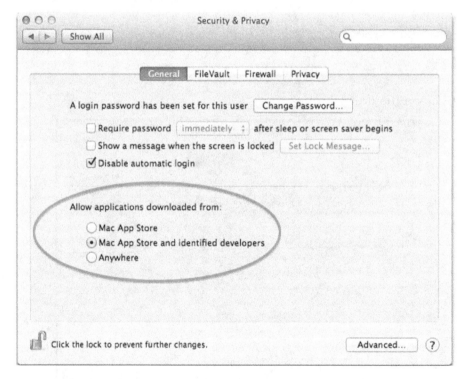

You'll need to click the padlock on the bottom left and enter your administrator username and password to access the settings.

Select the 'mac app store' selector to only allow apps from the app store.

250

Do Apple Macs get Viruses?

Yes they do! The likelihood of a Mac getting a virus when compared to a Windows user is less, since there are more Windows users than Mac users. Although MacOS is more secure than many versions of Windows, it still has its own security vulnerabilities.

As Macs become more popular, more and more malware is being developed to target MacOS. Even though Macs are more secure, make sure you are protected, as you can still be a victim of trojan horses, phishing, ransomware and other online fraud.

So don't fall victim to the 'macs don't get viruses' myth. Hackers and cyber thieves aren't after your computer, they're after your personal information so they can steal your identity, pin numbers and bank or credit card details. They'll try and trick you into handing this information over by pretending to be your bank, the IRS, or someone in authority. No super secure Mac is going to protect you against that.

A free simple anti virus for mac is Avast. There are a lot of different ones out there, but this one is free, small, fast and up to date so is a good place to start. It has a web shield to help protect you when you are browsing the web and warns you about websites that may have been compromised or reported as fake or fraudulent. It also has a email shield that scans incoming emails for worms and other threats.

You can download it here.

www.avast.com/mac

Once on their website, click the orange 'download' link.

Click 'download now' from the screen that appears.

Go to the downloads folder in your finder and double click on the following file.

```
avast_free_mac_security_online.dmg
```

In the finder window that appears, double click on 'avast security' to install.

Follow the instructions on screen.

Downloading MacOS Mojave

At the time of writing, you can download MacOS Mojave free of charge from the App Store and upgrade your Mac automatically.

Go to the App Store and click the download link. If it isn't on the home page you can search for it. Type in 'macos Mojave'.

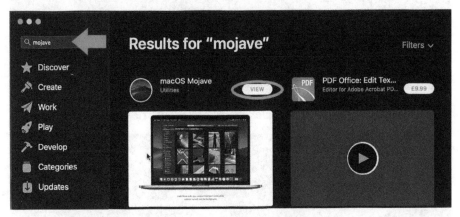

Click on 'view' next to 'macOS Mojave'. On the details page click 'get' to start downloading Mojave.

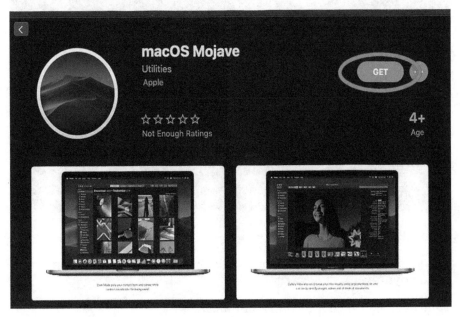

This download will take some time as it is about 5GB.

Installing MacOS Mojave

Once you have downloaded the installer from the app store, you will be able to find it in finder/applications.

Click finder on the bottom left of your dock, then select 'Applications'.

Double click the installer circled above to start the installer.

Follow the instructions on screen.

The installation will take a while. This is automated so you don't need to do anything.

Your mac may reboot a couple of times.

Once MacOS has installed, you'll need to run through the initial setup covered in 'starting your mac for the first time' section in chapter 2.

Create a Boot Drive

Creating a boot drive or recovery drive is always a good idea in case your mac crashes or your hard drive fails.

There is a very useful utility available on the internet, that will automatically create a boot drive on a USB memory stick or USB/Flash drive.

Open safari web browser and go to the following website

diskmakerx.com

Scroll down the page and click the link 'download diskmaker x'

Once you have downloaded the utility, go to your downloads folder and run the following application...

DiskMaker_X_8.dmg

...and follow the on screen instructions.

Chapter 7: Maintaining your Mac

For this utility to work, you'll need to first download MacOS Mojave from the app store, and have a flash drive that has at least 8GB available. Note that the diskmaker app will erase everything on the flash drive, so make sure it's one you don't use or have any important files on.

Open finder and go applications. Double click 'DiskMaker X'.

Select the version of Mac OS. Select the latest version available, either High Sierra (10.13) or Mojave (10.14).

Click 'select an OS X Installation App...'

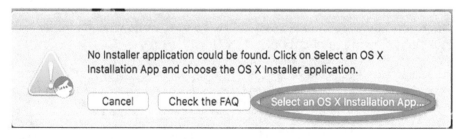

Browse to your applications folder and select the Mac OS Mojave Installer, circled below. Then click 'choose'.

Click 'use 8GB USB thumb drive'

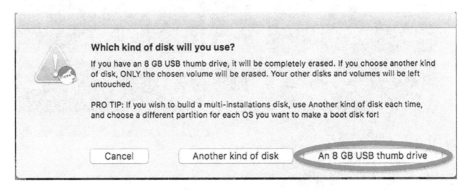

Wait for the utility to create your installer.

DiskMaker X will prompt you with a notification once your drive is ready for use. It will take a while to copy the required files.

Booting from a USB Drive

Now, to boot your Mac from the flash drive, insert the drive into a USB port and restart your mac.

When you hear the start up chime, hold down the Alt or Option key on your keyboard.

This will bring up the start up options menu.

Select your USB drive from the start up options.

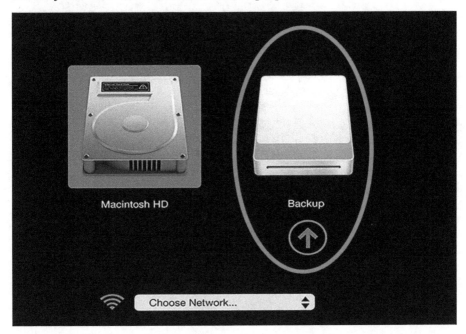

Now you'll need to run through the set up procedure. Hit 'continue', and follow the on screen instructions.

Agree to the terms and conditions. Click 'agree'.

Select the disk you want to install Mojave onto. This is usually your system disk and is already selected. Click 'install'.

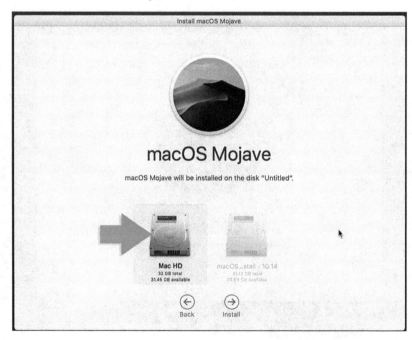

Now, if you have a time machine backup, plug in your external drive, and select 'restore from time machine backup', otherwise click 'install macos' to install a brand new system from scratch. Click 'continue'.

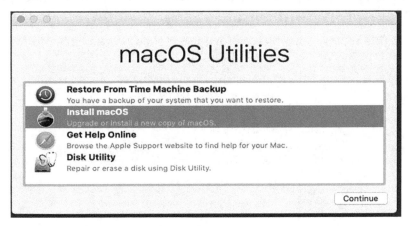

If you selected 'restore from time machine backup', select your time machine backup disk from the list, then select the latest backup from the list.

Follow the instructions on the screen to finish installing MacOS Mojave. Your Mac will restart itself a few times...

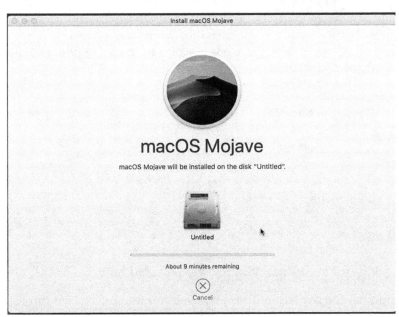

You'll need to run through 'starting your mac for the first time' in chapter 2.

Recovery Mode

If you need to reinstall MacOS or recover your Mac from a backup, you can boot into recovery mode.

To do this restart your Mac or turn it on. Hold down CMD and R.

Here you can reinstall MacOS, restore from a time machine backup or repair a disk with the disk utility.

App Updates

To check if there are any updates for apps you have installed, open the app store and select the 'updates' option from the panel on the left hand side of the screen.

If any updates are available, they will be listed here.

To apply all the available updates, click 'update all' on the top right of the screen.

To apply updates to individual apps, click 'update' next to the update in the list.

System Updates

System updates such as security updates and macos updates, have been moved to its own section in the system preferences app

If there are any updates available, they will be listed here. Click 'update now' to apply the updates.

Select 'automatically keep my mac up to date' and MacOS will automatically apply the updates in the background. Select 'advanced' to select which updates to apply automatically.

Select them all, then click 'ok'. This will ensure your mac is always up to date and it will do this in the background without prompting you.

SMC

The SMC or System Management Controller, and is responsible for controlling the power button, battery and temperature control of internal components, keyboard backlight, video sources and various status indicators.

If your Mac doesn't respond if you press the power button even if it's plugged in, shuts down unexpectedly or is generally running slowly, you can perform an SMC reset.

To do this, first shut down your Mac.

On your keyboard, Hold down:

Left Shift, Left Control, Left Option and the Power Button

Hold these at the same time for 10 seconds.

Some of the new Macs, you'll need to hold down the Right Shift, Left Control, and Left Option Key with the power button for 7 seconds.

Release all the keys, then press the power button to start your Mac as normal.

NVRAM

NVRAM or Non-volatile Random Access Memory, is a small memory chip that your Mac uses to store sound volume, display resolution, startup-disk selection, time zone, and other settings.

First, shut down your Mac.

Press the power button to start your Mac, then quickly hold down:

Option, Command, P, and R

You can release the keys after about 20 seconds, during which your Mac might appear to restart. You might hear two start up chimes.

Release the keys after you hear the second chime or see the Apple logo.

Video Resources

To help you understand the procedures and concepts explored in this book, we have developed some video resources and app demos for you to use, as you work through the book.

As well as the video resources, you'll also find some downloadable files and samples for exercises that appear in the book.

To find the resources, open your web browser and navigate to the following website

www.elluminetpress.com/resources/mac-os/

At the beginning of each chapter, you'll find a website that contains the resources for that chapter.

When you open the link to the video resources, you'll see a thumbnail list at the bottom.

Click on the thumbnail for the particular video you want to watch. Most videos are between 30 and 60 seconds outlining the procedure, others are a bit longer.

When the video is playing, hover your mouse over the video and you'll see some controls...

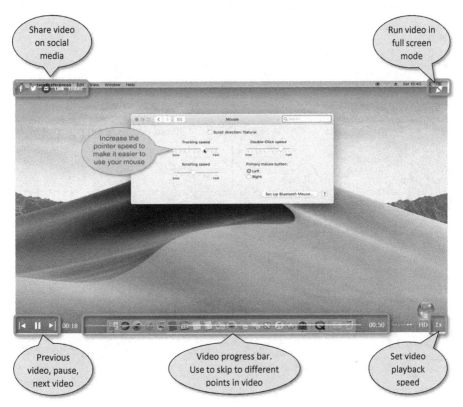

Appendix A: Video Resources

To save the files into your Mac, right click on the icons above and select 'download linked file as'.

In the dialog box that appears, click the down arrow to show the full dialog box.

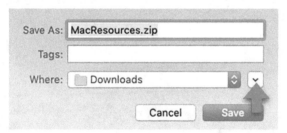

Select the folder you want to save the download into. Use 'pictures'.

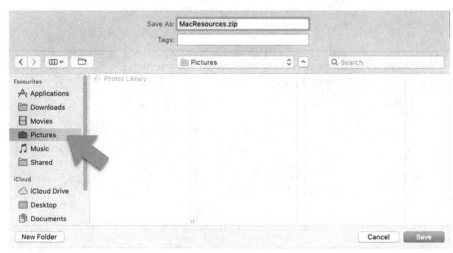

Click 'save'.

Once you have downloaded the zip file, open finder and go to your 'pictures' folder. Double click on the zip file to extract all the files.

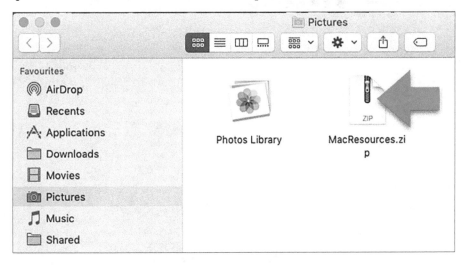

This will create a new folder in your pictures called 'Macs Resources'.

Double click to open this folder. You'll find the images used in the examples in the book.

Index

A

Accounts 42
  Adding Internet 42
  Additional Users 44
Address Book 177
Adjusting Photos
  Brightness 195
  White Balance 196
Air Drop 186
Apple Books 124
  Download Books 126
Apple Keys 33
Apple Music 242
  Adding Songs 247
  Browse 245
  Creating Playlists 247
  Recommendations 246
  Search 244
Apple Pay 91
  Setup 91
  Using Apple Pay on your Mac 94
Application Menu 55
App Store 118
App Updates 262
Auto Unlock 95

B

Backup
  Restoring Items 39

Setting Up Backups 35
Backup Files 35
Backups 35
Bluetooth 113
Blu-Ray 66
Blu-rays 136
Books 124
Boot Drive 255
  Create a Boot Drive 255
Booting from a USB Drive 258
Burn a Playlist to a CD 237

C

Calendar App 129
  Add an Event from Email 130
  Adding an Event 129
  Public Calendars 131
  Sharing Calendars 132
Camera 224
CDs 66
Changing Desktop Background 85
Clipboard 88
Close a Window 78
Cloud 34
Command Key 33
Compress Files 64
Contacts 177
  Add a Contact from Scratch 178
  Add Email Contact from Apple Mail 180
  Creating Groups 179
Continuity Camera 224
Control Key 33
Creating an Apple ID 34

D

Dark Mode 110
Dashboard 79
Desktop 49
Dock 51
Downloading Mojave 253
Downloading Sample Resources 266
DVDs 66, 136
Dynamic Desktop 85
  Change Background 85

Index

E

Ethernet 28
External Drives 65

F

Facetime 181
  Making a Call 181
Finder 56
  Markup 61
  Quick Preview Files 64
  Smart Folders 63
  Tabs & Tags 57
  View Style 59
Find my Mac 111
Firewalls 249
Frozen Apps 117
Function Key 33

G

Gatekeeper 250
Gestures 100
  Four Finger Open 102
  One Finger Point and Tap 100
  Two Finger Rotate 101
  Two Finger Scroll 101
  Two Finger Swipe 102

H

Handoff 86
HotSpot 89

I

iBooks 124
iCal 129
iCloud Drive 70
  File Sharing 73
iMac 16
iMac Pro 17
Image Capture 133
iMessage 184
iMovie 226
  Adding Clips 229
  Animations 233
  Importing Footage from your Camera 226
  Importing Footage from your iPhone 227
  Music 231

Titles 230
Transitions 232
Initial Setup 21
Installing Mojave 254
Internet Accounts 42
iTunes 234
  Add Music to iPhone or iPad 236
  Burn a Playlist to a CD 237
  Import from a CD 238
  Plugging in an iPhone or iPad 235
iTunes Store 239
  Films & TV Programmes 240
  Searching the Store 239

K

Keyboard 97
Keyboard Shortcuts 98
Keynote App 150
  Adding a New Slide 151
  Adding Media 152
  Adding Styles to Textboxes 156
  Animations 153
  Editing a Slide 151
  Formatting Text Boxes 154
  Formatting Text Inside Textboxes 155
  Saving 158

L

Launching Apps 53, 115
Launchpad 53
Locating your Mac & Taking Action 112
Lost Mac 111

M

Macbook 16
MacBook Air 16
Mac Mini 17
Mac Pro 17
Mail 169
  Attachment 171
  Emoji 171
  Formatting your Message 170
  Junk Mail 176
  Mail Drop 172
  Markup 174
  Photo from Photos App 172

Index

Writing an Email 170
Maps 121
  3D 123
  Directions 121
  GPS 123
Maximise a Window 78
Menu Bar 55
  Application Menu 55
  Status Menu 55
Minimise a Window 78
Mission Control 54
Models 16
  iMac 16
  iMac Pro 17
  Macbooks 16
  Mac Mini 17
  Mac Pro 17
Mouse 103
  Find your Mouse Pointer 105
  Left Click 103
  Right Click 103
  Scrolling 104
  Swipe 104
Moving a Window 76
Multimedia 188

N

Network 68
News App 142
Notes 127
Notification Centre 81
  Alerts 83
  Badges 83
  Banners 83
  Settings 84
Numbers App 159
  Building a Spreadsheet 161
  Changing Data Types 162
  Entering Data 161
  Formulas 162
  Functions 163
  Saving 163
NVRAM 265

O

Option Key 33

P

Pages App 144
  Adding a Picture 147
  Formatting Text 146
  Instant Alpha 148
  Saving 149
Peripherals 29
Phishing 251
Phone 187
Photobooth 134
Photos App 189
  Adding Photos to Albums 194
  Create your Own Memory 219
  Creating Folders and Albums 192
  Enhancing Photos 195
  Faces & Places 217
  Filters 198
  Gift Calendar 215
  Greeting Cards 212
  Importing 190
  Memories 219
  Ordering Prints 208
  Photobooks 201
  Printing Photos 210
  Share a Memory 222
  Sharing Photos 199
  Slide Shows 205
  Smart Search 223
Places 218
Power Down 20
Power Up 19
Printers 31

R

Ransomware 251
Recovery Mode 262
Resizing a Window 77
Resources 266

S

Safari 165
  Bookmarking Pages 166
  Downloads 168

Index

Launching Safari 165
Organise Bookmarks 168
Searching the Web 166
Sidebar 167
Search 80
Shared Folders 67
Sharing Files on a Network 68
Siri 90
SMC 264
Spaces 54
Spam 176
Spotlight 80
Stacks 50
Startup Keys 99
Status Menu 55
System Preferences 40
System Updates 263

T

Tabbed Apps 120
Tethering 89
Text Message 184
Time Machine Backup 35
Restoring Items 39
Setting Up Backups 35
Touch Bar 106
Application Strip 107
Control Strip 107
Customise 109
Layout 106
Trackpad 100
Four Finger Open Launchpad 102
One Finger Point and Tap 100
Two Finger Rotate 101
Two Finger Scroll 101
Two Finger Swipe 102
Trackpads 46

U

Universal Clipboard 88
Unresponsive Apps 117
Updates 262
USB-C ports 29

V

Video Resources 266
Virtual Desktops 54
Viruses 251
Voice Memos 138
  Recording Memos 139
  Renaming Memos 140
  Trim a Memo 141

W

Web Browser 165
WiFi 26